# The Galveston Diet

1500 Days of Easy and Fast Recipes a Vibrant and Balanced Life, Fresh and Seasonal Ingredients to Burn Fat and control Hormones | **Ready in less than 30 min**

for Beginners

**NAOMI LANE**

" Thank you.
This cookbook is dedicated to
my family and all your families.

Enjoy! "

# Contents

# Introduction

Step into the vibrant world of nutrition and wellness with the Galveston Diet, an innovative approach that combines science, nourishment, and the art of balanced living. Embark on a transformative journey that redefines the way you view food, empowering you to achieve optimal health and vitality.

The Galveston Diet invites you to embrace a lifestyle that is as enriching as the coastal city from which it draws its name. Just as the waves sculpt the shore, this revolutionary dietary method shapes your well-being, allowing you to sculpt a healthier, happier you.

Guided by the wisdom of Dr. Mary Claire Haver, a visionary leader in the field of women's health, the Galveston Diet offers a refreshing perspective on nutrition. It celebrates the unique needs of women and recognizes the delicate interplay between hormones, metabolism, and overall wellness. With her expertise and compassionate approach, Dr. Haver will guide you towards sustainable and long-lasting results.

Prepare to experience a symphony of flavors and nourishment as the Galveston Diet unveils a plethora of wholesome and delicious foods. From colorful vegetables and lean proteins to the delicate dance of spices and herbs, every meal becomes a celebration of health, delighting both your taste buds and your body.

But the Galveston Diet is more than just a collection of recipes—it's a mindset. It encourages you to honor your body, listen to its cues, and find joy in nourishing yourself. Embrace mindful eating, self-care, and the cultivation of a positive relationship with food as you embark on this transformative journey.

With the Galveston Diet, your health goals become a reality as you shed unwanted pounds, boost your energy levels, and rejuvenate your spirit. Join a community of empowered women who have embraced this path, supporting and inspiring one another as they embark on their unique wellness journeys.

Are you ready to unlock the full potential of your health? Welcome to the Galveston Diet—a nourishing voyage that will forever transform the way you nourish your body, mind, and soul.

## A brief overview of the Galveston Diet

### Definition
The Galveston Diet is a comprehensive weight loss approach specifically targeted towards women experiencing menopausal weight gain. It aims to counteract the effects of hormonal changes during menopause by incorporating a combination of anti-inflammatory foods and intermittent fasting. Unlike traditional calorie-restricted diets, the Galveston Diet prioritizes the consumption of anti-inflammatory foods, which are believed to promote fat loss by optimizing hormone function. The diet encourages whole foods while discouraging processed foods, added sugars, and artificial ingredients, thereby promoting a more balanced and healthful eating pattern.

By emphasizing anti-inflammatory foods and limiting the intake of processed and artificial foods, the Galveston Diet seeks to address the underlying hormonal imbalances that contribute to weight gain during menopause. This approach recognizes the importance of hormonal health in achieving sustainable weight loss and overall well-being. Through its emphasis on whole foods, the Galveston Diet encourages individuals to make healthier dietary choices that can support their weight loss goals and improve their overall health. Additionally, incorporating intermittent fasting into the program provides an additional tool for regulating calorie intake and potentially enhancing fat burning. Ultimately, the Galveston Diet offers a self-paced weight loss program tailored to women experiencing menopausal weight gain, with a focus on nourishing the body with anti-inflammatory foods and adopting intermittent fasting as part of a comprehensive approach in terms of achieving and maintaining a healthy weight.

**Purpose:**

1. Weight loss: The primary purpose of the Galveston Diet is to support and facilitate weight loss, particularly targeting menopausal weight gain. By incorporating anti-inflammatory foods and intermittent fasting, the diet aims to help women shed excess pounds.
2. Hormonal balance: The diet focuses on anti-inflammatory foods that can help regulate hormones, particularly during menopause. This can potentially alleviate symptoms such as hot flashes, mood swings, and sleep disturbances.
3. Anti-inflammatory effects: By emphasizing whole foods and minimizing processed foods, added sugars, and artificial ingredients, the Galveston Diet aims to reduce inflammation in the body. Chronic inflammation is associated with different health issues, including weight gain and increased risk of diseases.
4. Improved insulin sensitivity: The diet's emphasis on whole foods and intermittent fasting can help improve insulin sensitivity. This can be beneficial for managing blood sugar levels and preventing or managing conditions like insulin resistance and type 2 diabetes.
5. Increased energy levels: By providing nourishing foods and stabilizing blood sugar levels, the Galveston Diet can potentially increase energy levels and reduce fatigue often experienced during menopause.
6. Enhanced mental clarity: The diet's focus on whole, nutrient-dense foods can support brain health and cognitive function, potentially leading to improved mental clarity and focus.
7. Reduced cravings: The combination of anti-inflammatory foods and intermittent fasting can help regulate appetite and reduce cravings, making it

really easier to adhere to the diet and make healthier food choices.
8. Improved gut health: The emphasis on whole foods and the avoidance of processed foods can support a healthy gut microbiome. A balanced gut microbiome is associated with better digestion, nutrient absorption, and overall immune function.
9. Cardiovascular health: The Galveston Diet's focus on whole foods and anti-inflammatory ingredients may have a positive impact on heart health through the reduction of inflammation, improving lipid profiles, and managing blood pressure levels.
10. Long-term lifestyle change: While the Galveston Diet provides a structured plan, it also aims to promote long-term lifestyle changes. By encouraging the consumption of whole foods and limiting processed foods and added sugars, the diet promotes sustainable eating habits that can support overall health and weight management in the long run.

## Goals

The Galveston Diet is a popular weight loss and health program created by Dr. Mary Claire Haver, a board-certified OB-GYN and women's health expert. While I cannot provide an exhaustive list of 15 specific goals of the Galveston Diet, I can give you a general overview of the main objectives typically associated with this program. Here are some common goals of the Galveston Diet:

1. Weight loss: The primary goal of the Galveston Diet is to help individuals achieve sustainable weight loss by promoting healthy eating habits and lifestyle changes.
2. Hormonal balance: The diet aims to support hormonal balance, particularly in women going through perimenopause and menopause. It focuses on addressing issues such as insulin resistance and cortisol imbalances that can contribute to weight gain.

3. Reduced inflammation: The Galveston Diet emphasizes consuming anti-inflammatory foods and avoiding inflammatory foods, as chronic inflammation is associated with various health conditions.

4. Increased energy: By providing the body with the right nutrients and avoiding processed foods, the diet aims to improve energy levels and combat fatigue.

5. Improved sleep: The program recognizes the importance of quality sleep for overall health and weight management, offering strategies to improve sleep patterns.

6. Enhanced mental clarity: By prioritizing nutrient-dense foods and avoiding processed sugars, the Galveston Diet aims to support mental clarity and cognitive function.

7. Balanced blood sugar levels: The diet encourages stable blood sugar levels by emphasizing low-glycaemic index foods and portion control.

8. Reduced cravings: By focusing on whole, unprocessed foods, the Galveston Diet aims to minimize cravings for sugary and processed snacks.

9. Support for women's health: The program specifically caters to women's unique health concerns, including hormonal imbalances and menopause-related symptoms.

10. Lowered risk of chronic diseases: By promoting a healthy diet and lifestyle, the Galveston Diet aims to reduce the risk of chronic conditions such as heart disease, diabetes, and certain cancers.

11. Improved gut health: The diet emphasizes the consumption of fiber-rich foods and probiotics to support a healthy gut microbiome.

12. Sustainable approach: The Galveston Diet aims to provide individuals with long-term tools and strategies to maintain a healthy weight and lifestyle beyond the initial weight loss phase.

13. Education and empowerment: The program educates participants about nutrition, hormonal health, and the importance of self-care, empowering them to make informed choices.

14. Supportive community: The Galveston Diet offers a community platform where participants can connect, share experiences, and receive support throughout their weight loss journey.

15. Individualized approach: The program recognizes that each person's body and needs are unique, and it aims to provide personalized guidance and support to help individuals achieve their health and weight goals.

## Founder of Galveston Diet

The Galveston Diet, spearheaded by the renowned doctor Mary Claire Haver, M.D., stands as a groundbreaking anti-inflammatory nutrition program and empowering community. With a specific focus on individuals navigating perimenopause, menopause, and the transformative years beyond, this revolutionary approach to wellness offers a beacon of hope. Driven by Dr. Haver's expertise and unwavering dedication, the Galveston Diet has emerged as a powerful resource for those seeking to optimize their health and well-being during this pivotal stage of life. By blending cutting-edge research, personalized nutritional guidance, and a supportive community, the Galveston Diet empowers individuals to embrace vibrant living, rediscover their vitality, and truly thrive.

## Benefits of Galveston Diet

The Galveston Diet is a popular anti-inflammatory nutrition program that specifically targets women in perimenopause, menopause, and beyond. Here are 15 potential benefits of following the Galveston Diet:

1. Hormonal balance: The diet aims to support hormonal balance during the transition into menopause, which can help alleviate common symptoms like hot flashes, mood swings, and weight gain.

2. Reduced inflammation: The Galveston Diet focuses on reducing inflammation, which can contribute to various health

issues, including joint pain, digestive problems, and chronic diseases.

3. Weight management: Following the Galveston Diet can aid in weight management, as it emphasizes nutrient-dense foods and portion control.

4. Increases energy levels: By nourishing your body with balanced meals and avoiding inflammatory foods, you may experience increases in energy levels and improved overall vitality.

5. Improved sleep quality: The diet's emphasis on anti-inflammatory foods and balanced meals can contribute to better sleep quality, which is crucial for overall health and well-being.

6. Reduced bloating and digestive discomfort: The Galveston Diet promotes a gut-friendly approach, which may reduce bloating, gas, and other digestive discomforts commonly experienced during perimenopause and menopause.

7. Better skin health: The anti-inflammatory nature of the diet can potentially improve skin health, reducing issues like acne, redness, and inflammation.

8. Reduces risk of chronic diseases: By adopting an anti-inflammatory approach, the Galveston Diet may help reduce the risk of developing chronic diseases like heart disease, diabetes, and certain cancers.

9. Enhanced cognitive function: Some studies suggest that an anti-inflammatory diet can support brain health, potentially enhancing cognitive function and reducing the risk of age-related cognitive decline.

10. Balanced blood sugar levels: The Galveston Diet encourages balanced meals and reduces the consumption of processed sugars, which can help stabilize blood sugar levels and prevent insulin spikes.

11. Improved mood and mental well-being: The diet's focus on nutrient-dense foods and hormonal balance can positively impact mood and mental well-being, reducing symptoms of depression, anxiety, and irritability.

12. Reduced risk of osteoporosis: The Galveston Diet emphasizes calcium-rich foods, which can support bone health and reduce the risk of osteoporosis, a common concern during menopause.

13. Enhanced cardiovascular health: By reducing inflammation and promoting a balanced diet, the Galveston Diet may contribute to improved cardiovascular health, including lower blood pressure and cholesterol levels.

14. Balanced and sustainable eating habits: The program promotes long-term lifestyle changes rather than short-term dieting, helping individuals develop balanced and sustainable eating habits.

15. Supportive community: The Galveston Diet includes a community aspect, providing support, motivation, and accountability to its members, which can contribute to overall success and adherence to the program.

## Recommended foods

The Galveston Diet emphasizes whole, nutrient-dense foods that reduce inflammation and support overall health. By incorporating these recommended foods into one's eating plan, individuals can experience the benefits of improved hormone balance, reduced menopausal weight gain, and increased overall well-being.

1. Berries: Berries, such as strawberries, blueberries, and raspberries, are rich in antioxidants and fiber. They help combat inflammation and provide essential vitamins and minerals. Their low glycemic index also helps stabilize blood sugar levels, making them quite an excellent choice for the Galveston Diet.

2. Leafy Greens: Leafy greens like spinach, kale, and Swiss chard are packed with nutrients and are low in calories. They are a great source of vitamins A and C along with minerals that includecalcium and iron. The high fiber content aids in terms of digestion

and promotes a healthy gut, while their antioxidants help reduce inflammation.

3. Salmon: Rich in omega-3 fatty acids, salmon is a richsource of lean protein and healthy fats. These fatty acids have anti-inflammatory properties and support brain health. Salmon is also considered as an excellent source of vitamin D, which plays a crucial role in maintaining bone health and immune function.

4. Lentils: Legumes like lentils are high in fiber, protein, and complex carbohydrates. They provide a steady release of energy and help keep you feeling full and satisfied. Lentils also contain phytochemicals that have anti-inflammatory properties, making them a great addition to the Galveston Diet.

5. Quinoa: Quinoa is a nutritious whole grain that is rich in protein and fiber. It contains essential amino acids and is gluten-free. Quinoa provides a sustained release of energy, helps stabilize blood sugar levels, and is a good source of vitamins and minerals.

6. Olive Oil: Olive oil is a type of healthy fat that is considered rich in monounsaturated fats as well as antioxidants. It has been associated with a reduced risk of heart disease and inflammation. Incorporating olive oil into your diet can be beneficial for overall health and is a great choice for cooking and dressing salads.

7. Nuts and Seeds: Nuts and seeds like almonds, walnuts, chia seeds, and flaxseeds, are packed with nutrients, including healthy fats, fiber, and protein. They provide a satisfying crunch to meals and snacks while offering anti-inflammatory benefits and promoting heart health.

8. Greek Yogurt: Full-fat Greek yogurt is a good source of protein and calcium. It contains beneficial probiotics that support gut health and may reduce inflammation. Choosing full-fat dairy over low-fat or fat-free options is a part of the Galveston Diet, as it helps promote satiety and hormone balance.

9. Turmeric: Turmeric is a spice with potent anti-inflammatory properties due to its active compound called curcumin. Adding turmeric to your meals can help reduce inflammation and provide antioxidant benefits. It can be used in various dishes, such as curries, soups, and smoothies.

10. Dark Chocolate: Dark chocolate with a high cocoa content (70% or more) is rich in antioxidants and flavonoids. It has been connected with a lower risk of heart disease and reduced inflammation. Consuming a moderate amount of dark chocolate can be a satisfying and indulgent treat while following the Galveston Diet.

## Foods not Allowed:

The Galveston Diet is a popular eating plan that focuses on reducing inflammation and balancing hormones to promote weight loss and overall health. As part of this diet, certain foods are restricted due to their potential to cause inflammation and disrupt hormonal balance. Here are 10 foods not allowed in the Galveston Diet, along with a paragraph explanation for each:

**Most processed foods:**
Processed foods often contain unhealthy additives, preservatives, and high levels of sodium. They are typically low in nutrients and high in calories, contributing to weight gain and inflammation.

**Fried foods:**
Fried foods are typically cooked in unhealthy oils that are high in trans fats and saturated fats. These fats can contribute to inflammation, increase the risk of heart disease, as well as promote weight gain.

**Artificial ingredients, colors, or flavors:**
Artificial additives like artificial sweeteners, colors, and flavors can trigger inflammation and disrupt hormonal balance. They are commonly found in processed foods, sodas, and sweet treats.

Foods with added sugars: Foods with added sugars, such as desserts, sugary beverages, and processed snacks, can lead to weight gain, insulin resistance, and inflammation. They provide empty calories and lack beneficial nutrients.

**High fructose corn syrup:**
High fructose corn syrup is a common sweetener found in many processed foods and beverages. It has been linked to obesity, insulin resistance, and inflammation, making it a food to avoid in the Galveston Diet.

**Processed meats with nitrates/nitrites:**
Processed meats like sausages, hot dogs, and deli meats often contain nitrates and nitrites, which are preservatives linked to an increased risk of certain cancers. They can also contribute to inflammation.

**Refined flours and refined grains:**
Refined flours and grains, such as white bread, pasta, and white rice, have been stripped of their fiber and nutrients. They have a high glycemic index, leading to rapid spikes in blood sugar levels, inflammation, and weight gain.

**Canola or vegetable oil:**
Canola and certain vegetable oils are high in omega-6 fatty acids, which, when consumed in excess, can promote inflammation in the body. It is best to opt for healthier oils like olive oil or avocado oil.

**Artificial sweeteners:**
Artificial sweeteners, such as aspartame, sucralose, and saccharin, may disrupt gut health, trigger cravings for sweet foods, and contribute to inflammation. They are commonly found in diet sodas and sugar-free products.

**Alcohol:**
While moderate alcohol consumption may have some health benefits, excessive alcohol intake can disrupt hormonal balance, hinder weight loss efforts, and promote inflammation. It is recommended to limit or even avoid alcohol on the Galveston Diet.

# Breakfast Recipes

## Beet & Berries Smoothie Bowl

**Serving Portion:** 1 | **Preparation Period:** 10 mins. | **Cooking Period:** 10 mins.

**Ingredients Required:**

**For the Smoothie Bowl:**

- 1 C. beets, peel removed and cut up
- 1 C. strawberries (fresh)
- ¼ C. cranberries (fresh)
- 1 scoop vanilla protein powder
- ½ C. almond milk (unsweetened)
- 4 ice cubes

**For the Topping:**

- ¼ C. mixed berries (blueberries, raspberries)
- 1 tsp. unsweetened coconut, shredded

**Procedure of Cooking:**

1. For smoothie bowl: Put in beets and remnant ingredients in a high-power mixer and process to form a smooth mixture.
2. Enjoy immediately with topping ingredients.

**Nutritional Facts:**
Calories: 294 | Fat: 4.3g | Carbs: 35.4g | Protein: 30.1g

## Fruity Greens Smoothie Bowl

**Serving Portions:** 2 | **Preparation Period:** 10 mins.

**Ingredients Required:**

- 1 C. strawberries (fresh)

- 2 medium-sized ripe frozen bananas, peel removed and slivered
- ¼ of ripe avocado, peel removed, pitted and cut up
- 1 C. spinach (fresh)
- 1 C. kale (fresh), tough ribs removed
- 1 tbsp. flaxseed meal
- 1½ C. almond milk (unsweetened)

**Procedure of Cooking:**

1. In a high-power mixer, put in strawberries and remnant ingredients and process to form a smooth mixture.
2. Enjoy immediately with your favorite topping.

**Nutritional Facts:**
Calories: 225 | Fat: 7.2g | Carbs: 40.2g | Protein: 4.9g

## Fruity Yogurt Bowl

**Serving Portions:** 2 | **Preparation Period:** 10 mins.

**Ingredients Required:**

- 1 C. fat-free plain Greek yogurt
- 2 tsp. maple syrup
- ½ C. peaches, pitted and cut up
- ½ C. raspberries (fresh)
- ¼ C. blueberries (fresh)
- ¼ C. cherries (fresh), pitted
- 2 tbsp. macadamia nuts, crushed

**Procedure of Cooking:**

1. In a large-sized bowl, put in yogurt.
2. Put in maple syrup, fruit and macadamia nuts and lightly blend to incorporate.
3. Enjoy immediately.

**Nutritional Facts:**
Calories: 168| Fat: 6.8g| Carbs: 22.1g| Protein: 6.8g

## Granola Yogurt Bowl

**Serving Portions:** 4| **Preparation Period:** 10 mins.

**Ingredients Required:**

- ½ C. strawberries (fresh), slivered
- ¼ C. blueberries (fresh)
- ¼ C. raspberries (fresh)
- 2½ C. fat-free plain Greek yogurt, divided
- ½ C. crunchy maple granola

**Procedure of Cooking:**

1. In a medium-sized bowl, blend all together berries.
2. In 4 serving bowls, divide the yogurt.
3. Decorate with berries and granola and enjoy immediately.

**Nutritional Facts:**
Calories: 125| Fat: 7.5g| Carbs: 30.5g| Protein: 12.3g

## Oatmeal Yogurt Bowl

**Serving Portions:** 2| **Preparation Period:** 10 mins.| **Cooking Period:** 10 mins.

**Ingredients Required:**

- 2 C. water
- 1 C. gluten-free old-fashioned oats
- 6 oz. non-fat plain Greek yogurt
- ½ C. strawberries (fresh)

**Procedure of Cooking:**

1. In a small-sized saucepan, put in water on burner at around medium heat.
2. Cook the water until boiling.

3. Blend in the oats.
4. Cook for around 5 minutes, mixing time to time.
5. Take off the pan of oats from burner and blend in half of the yogurt and cinnamon.
6. Divide the oatmeal into serving bowls.
7. Top each bowl with strawberry slices and enjoy.

**Nutritional Facts:**
Calories: 210| Fat: 3.1g| Carbs: 37.6g| Protein: 9.8g

## Fruity Chia Pudding

**Serving Portions:** 4| **Preparation Period:** 10 mins.

**Ingredients Required:**

- 2/3 C. almond milk (unsweetened)
- 2 C. frozen blueberries
- ½ of frozen banana, peel removed and slivered
- 5 large soft dates, pitted and cut up
- ½ C. chia seeds

**Procedure of Cooking:**

1. Put in almond milk and fruit in a food mixer and process to form a smooth mixture.
2. Shift the mixture into a bowl.
3. Put in chia seeds and blend to incorporate thoroughly.
4. Shift into your refrigerator for 30 minutes, mixing after every 5 minutes.

**Nutritional Facts:**
Calories: 149| Fat: 5.9g| Carbs: 28g| Protein: 4.1g

## Microwave Oatmeal

**Serving Portions:** 2| **Preparation Period:** 10 mins.| **Cooking Period:** 3 mins.

**Ingredients Required:**

- 2/3 C. coconut milk (unsweetened)
- ½ C. gluten-free quick-cooking oats
- ½ tsp. powdered cinnamon
- ½ tsp. powdered turmeric
- ¼ tsp. powdered ginger

**Procedure of Cooking:**

1. In a microwave-safe bowl, blend all together milk and oats.
2. Microwave on high setting for around 1 minute.
3. Take off from microwave and blend in the spices.
4. Microwave on high for around 2 minutes, mixing after every 20 seconds.
5. Enjoy immediately.

**Nutritional Facts:**
Calories: 202 | Fat: 12.4g | Carbs: 16.8g | Protein: 3.8g

## Overnight Oatmeal

**Serving Portions:** 2 | **Preparation Period:** 10 mins.

**Ingredients Required:**

- 1 C. gluten-free rolled oats
- ½ tsp. powdered cinnamon
- 2 tsp. honey
- 1 C. almond milk (unsweetened)
- ¼ C. blueberries (fresh)

**Procedure of Cooking:**

1. In a large-sized bowl, put in oats, cinnamon, honey and almond milk and blend to incorporate thoroughly.
2. Cover the bowl and shift into your refrigerator all the night.
3. In the morning, decorate with blueberries and enjoy.

**Nutritional Facts:**
Calories: 203 | Fat: 4.4g | Carbs: 36.9g | Protein: 5.9g

## Quinoa Porridge

**Serving Portions:** 4 | **Preparation Period:** 10 mins. | **Cooking Period:** 15 mins.

**Ingredients Required:**

- 2 C. water
- 1 C. dry quinoa, rinsed
- ½ tsp. vanilla essence
- ½ C. almond milk (unsweetened)
- 3-4 tbsp. honey
- ¼ tsp. fresh lemon peel, finely grated
- ½ tsp. powdered ginger
- ½ tsp. powdered cinnamon
- ½ tsp. powdered nutmeg
- 1 pinch of powdered cloves
- 1 C. apple, cored and slivered

**Procedure of Cooking:**

1. In a medium-sized saucepan, blend all together water, quinoa and vanilla essence on burner at around low heat.
2. Cook for around 10-15 minutes, mixing time to time.
3. Put in almond milk, honey, lemon peel and spices and blend to incorporate thoroughly.
4. Immediately take off from burner.
5. Decorate with apple slices and enjoy.

**Nutritional Facts:**
Calories: 195 | Fat: 3.2g | Carbs: 35.9g | Protein: 6.7g

## Milk Crepes

**Serving Portions:** 4 | **Preparation Period:** 15 mins. | **Cooking Period:** 16 mins.

**Ingredients Required:**

- 1 C. whole-wheat flour

- 1/8 tsp. salt
- 2 eggs
- ½ C. fat-free milk
- ½ C. water
- 1 tbsp. olive oil

**Procedure of Cooking:**

1. In a large-sized bowl, blend all together flour and salt.
2. Put in eggs and blend to incorporate thoroughly.
3. Slowly Put in milk and water and whisk to incorporate thoroughly.
4. In an anti-sticking wok, sizzle the oil on burner at around medium-high heat.
5. Put in about ¼ C. of the mixture and spread in a thin layer.
6. Cook for around 2 minutes.
7. Carefully change the side of crepe.
8. Cook for around 1-2 minutes.
9. Cook the remnant crepes in the same manner.
10. Enjoy warm.

**Nutritional Facts:**
Calories: 171| Fat: 6.2g| Carbs: 22.8g| Protein: 7.8g

## Banana Pancakes

**Serving Portions:** 5| **Preparation Period:** 15 mins.| **Cooking Period:** 25 mins.

**Ingredients Required:**

- ¼ C. coconut flour
- ¼ tsp. baking powder
- ½ tsp. powdered cinnamon
- 1 pinch of salt
- ½ C. almond milk (unsweetened)
- 2 eggs
- 1 ripe banana, peel removed and mashed
- 1 tbsp. unsweetened applesauce
- 1 tsp. apple cider vinegar
- ½ tsp. vanilla extract
- 2 tsp. olive oil

**Procedure of Cooking:**

1. In a large-sized bowl, put in flour, baking powder, cinnamon and salt and blend to incorporate thoroughly.
2. In a separate bowl, put in almond milk, egg, banana, applesauce, vinegar and vanilla and whisk to incorporate thoroughly.
3. Put in egg mixture into the bowl of flour mixture and blend to incorporate thoroughly.
4. In a large-sized frying pan, sizzle the oil on burner at around medium heat.
5. Put in desired amount of mixture and spread in an even layer.
6. Cook for around 2-3 minutes.
7. Change the side of pancake.
8. Cook for around 1-2 minutes more.
9. Cook the remnant pancakes in the same manner.
10. Enjoy warm.

**Nutritional Facts:**
Calories: 94| Fat: 4.7g| Carbs: 10.4g| Protein: 3.4g

## Egg White Waffles

**Serving Portions:** 2| **Preparation Period:** 15 mins.| **Cooking Period:** 8 minutes

**Ingredients Required:**

- ¼ C. coconut flour
- 1 tsp. baking powder
- ¼ C. almond milk (unsweetened)
- 6 egg whites
- 1 tbsp. unsweetened applesauce
- Olive oil baking spray

**Procedure of Cooking:**

1. In a large-sized bowl, blend all together flour and baking powder.
2. Put in remnant ingredients and blend to incorporate thoroughly.
3. Preheat your waffle iron and then spray it with baking spray.

4. Place half of the mixture in preheated waffle iron.
5. Cook for around 3-4 minutes.
6. Cook the remnant waffles in the same manner.
7. Enjoy warm.

**Nutritional Facts:**
Calories: 123| Fat: 2.1g| Carbs: 13g| Protein: 12.9g

## Kale Scramble

**Serving Portions:** 2| **Preparation Period:** 10 mins.| **Cooking Period:** 6 minutes

**Ingredients Required:**

- 4 eggs
- 2 tbsp. coconut oil
- 2 C. kale (fresh), tough ribs removed and cut up
- 1½ tsp. powdered turmeric
- 1 tsp. garlic powder
- Salt and powdered black pepper, as desired

**Procedure of Cooking:**

1. In a small-sized bowl, put in eggs and whisk thoroughly. Put it aside.
2. In an anti-sticking wok, sizzle coconut oil on burner at around medium heat.
3. Cook the kale for around 2 minutes.
4. Put in eggs and remnant ingredients.
5. Cook for around 3-4 minutes, mixing all the time.
6. Enjoy immediately.

**Nutritional Facts:**
Calories: 258| Fat: 22.5g| Carbs: 4.1g| Protein: 12g

## Veggie Omelet

**Serving Portions:** 4| **Preparation Period:** 15 mins.| **Cooking Period:** 25 minutes

**Ingredients Required:**

- Olive oil baking spray
- 6 large eggs
- ½ C. almond milk (unsweetened)
- Salt and powdered black pepper, as desired
- ½ onion, cut up
- ¼ C. bell pepper, seeds removed and cut up
- ¼ C. mushrooms (fresh), slivered
- 1 tbsp. chives, finely cut up

**Procedure of Cooking:**

1. For preheating: set your oven at 350ºF.
2. Lightly spray a pie dish with baking spray.
3. In a bowl, put in eggs, almond milk, salt and pepper and whisk to incorporate thoroughly.
4. In a separate bowl, blend all together onion, bell pepper and mushrooms.
5. Place the egg mixture into the pie dish and top with vegetable mixture.
6. Sprinkle with chives.
7. Bake in your oven for around 20-25 minutes.
8. Take off the pie dish from oven and cut into serving portions.
9. Enjoy immediately.

**Nutritional Facts:**
Calories: 121| Fat: 8g| Carbs: 2.8g| Protein: 10g

## Eggs with Spinach

**Serving Portions:** 2| **Preparation Period:** 10 mins.| **Cooking Period:** 22 mins.

**Ingredients Required:**

- Olive oil baking spray
- 6 C. fresh baby spinach
- 2-3 tbsp. water
- 4 eggs

- Salt and powdered black pepper, as desired
- 2-3 tbsp. feta cheese, crumbled

**Procedure of Cooking:**

1. For preheating: set your oven at 400°F.
2. Lightly spray 2 small-sized baking pans with baking spray.
3. In a large-sized frying pan, put in spinach and water on burner at around medium heat.
4. Cook for around 3-4 minutes.
5. Take off the frying pan from burner and drain the excess water thoroughly.
6. Divide the spinach into both baking pans.
7. Carefully crack 2 eggs in each baking pan over spinach.
8. Sprinkle with salt and pepper and top with feta cheese.
9. Lay out the baking pans onto a large-sized cookie tray.
10. Bake in your oven for around 15-18 minutes.
11. Enjoy warm.

**Nutritional Facts:**
Calories: 171| Fat: 11.1g| Carbs: 4.3g| Protein: 15g

## Mushroom & Arugula Frittata

**Serving Portions:** 6| **Preparation Period:** 15 mins.| **Cooking Period:** 25 mins.

**Ingredients Required:**

- ½ C. coconut milk (unsweetened)
- 12 large-sized eggs
- Salt, as desired
- 2 tbsp. coconut oil, divided
- 1 small-sized red onion, cut up finely
- 1 C. mushrooms (fresh), slivered
- 1 C. arugula (fresh), cut up

**Procedure of Cooking:**

1. For preheating: set your oven at 375°F.

2. In a medium-sized bowl, put in coconut milk, eggs and salt and whisk thoroughly. Put it aside.
3. In an ovenproof wok, sizzle 1½ tbsp. of oil on burner at around medium-high heat.
4. Cook the onion for around 3 minutes.
5. Put in mushrooms and blend.
6. Cook for around 4-5 minutes.
7. Put in arugula and blend.
8. Cook for around 2-3 minutes.
9. Shift the vegetable mixture into a bowl.
10. In the same wok, sizzle the remnant oil on burner at around medium-low heat.
11. Put in egg mixture and tilt the pan to spread the mixture.
12. Cook for around 5 minutes.
13. Spread the vegetable mixture over cooked egg mixture.
14. Immediately Shift the wok into oven and Bake in your oven for around 5 minutes.
15. Take off the wok from oven and carefully flip the frittata.
16. Bake in your oven for around 3-4 minutes more.
17. Take off the wok of frittata from oven and put it aside for around 5 minutes before enjoying.
18. Divide the frittata into serving wedges and enjoy.

**Nutritional Facts:**
Calories: 220| Fat: 17.3g| Carbs: 2.9g| Protein: 13.4g

## Blueberry Muffins

**Serving Portions:** 5| **Preparation Period:** 10 mins.| **Cooking Period:** 12 minutes

**Ingredients Required:**

- ½ C. rolled oats
- ¼ C. almond flour
- ½ tsp. baking soda
- 2 tbsp. flaxseeds
- ½ tsp. powdered cinnamon
- 1 pinch of powdered nutmeg

- 1 egg
- ¼ C. almond butter, softened
- 2 tbsp. banana, peel removed and slivered
- ½ tsp. vanilla extract
- ¼ C. blueberries (fresh)

**Procedure of Cooking:**

1. For preheating: set your oven at 375°F.
2. Spray 10 holes of a muffin tin.
3. In a mixer, put in oats and remnant ingredients except for blueberries and process to form a smooth mixture and creamy.
4. Shift the mixture into a bowl and lightly blend in blueberries.
5. Place the mixture into prepared muffin holes.
6. Bake in your oven for around 10-12 minutes.
7. Take off the muffin tin from oven and place onto a counter to cool for around 10 minutes.
8. Carefully take off the muffins from tin and shift onto a platter to cool thoroughly before enjoying.

**Nutritional Facts:**
Calories: 105 | Fat: 5.6g | Carbs: 9.9g | Protein: 4.2g

## Chicken & Bell Pepper Muffins

**Serving Portions:** 4 | **Preparation Period:** 15 mins. | **Cooking Period:** 20 mins.

**Ingredients Required:**

- 8 eggs
- Powdered black pepper, as desired
- 2 tbsp. water
- 8 oz. cooked chicken, cut up finely
- 1 C. bell pepper, seeds removed and cut up
- 1 C. onion, cut up

**Procedure of Cooking:**

1. For preheating: set your oven at 350°F.
2. Spray 8 holes of a muffin tin.
3. In a large-sized bowl, put in eggs, black pepper and water and whisk to incorporate thoroughly.
4. Put in chicken, bell pepper and onion and blend to incorporate.
5. Shift the mixture in prepared muffin holes.
6. Bake in your oven for around 18-20 minutes.
7. Take off the muffin tin from oven and place onto a counter to cool for around 10 minutes.
8. Carefully take off the muffins from tin and shift onto a platter.
9. Enjoy warm.

**Nutritional Facts:**
Calories: 232 | Fat: 10.6g | Carbs: 5.6g | Protein: 28.1g

## Quinoa Bread

**Serving Portions:** 12 | **Preparation Period:** 10 mins. | **Cooking Period:** 1½ hrs.

**Ingredients Required:**

- 1¾ C. uncooked quinoa, soaked all the night and rinsed
- ¼ C. chia seeds, soaked in ½ C. of water all the night
- ½ tsp. bicarbonate soda
- Salt, as desired
- ¼ C. olive oil
- ½ C. water
- 1 tbsp. lemon juice (fresh)

**Procedure of Cooking:**

1. For preheating: set your oven at 320°F.
2. Lay out bakery paper into a loaf pan.
3. In a clean food mixer, put in quinoa and remnant ingredients and process for around 3 minutes.
4. Place the mixture into the loaf pan.
5. Bake in your oven for around 1½ hours.

6. Take off the loaf pan from oven and place onto a counter to cool for at least 10-15 minutes.
7. Carefully take off the bread from pan and shift onto a platter to cool thoroughly.
8. Divide the bread loaf into serving slices and enjoy.

**Nutritional Facts:**
Calories: 137 | Fat: 6.5g | Carbs: 16.9g | Protein: 4g

# Carrot Bread

**Serving Portions:** 8 | **Preparation Period:** 15 mins. | **Cooking Period:** 1 hr.

**Ingredients Required:**

- 2 C. almond meal
- 1 tsp. baking powder
- 1 tbsp. cumin seeds
- Salt, as desired
- 3 eggs
- 2 tbsp. macadamia nut oil
- 1 tbsp. apple cider vinegar
- 3 C. carrot, peel removed and grated
- 1 (½-inch) piece ginger root (fresh), peel removed and grated
- ¼ C. sultanas

**Procedure of Cooking:**

1. For preheating: set your oven at 350°F.
2. Lay out bakery paper into a loaf pan.
3. In a large-sized bowl, blend all together almond meal, baking powder, cumin seeds and salt.
4. In another bowl, put in eggs, nut oil and vinegar and whisk to incorporate thoroughly.
5. Put in egg mixture into the flour mixture and blend to incorporate thoroughly.
6. Lightly blend in carrot, ginger and sultanas.
7. Shift the mixture into the loaf pan.
8. Bake in your oven for around 1 hour.
9. Take off the loaf pan from oven and place onto a counter to cool for at least 10-15 minutes.
10. Then invert the bread onto the platter to cool thoroughly.
11. Divide the bread loaf into serving slices and enjoy.

**Nutritional Facts:**
Calories: 238 | Fat: 19.2g | Carbs: 11.7g | Protein: 8.6g

# Salad Recipes

## Berries & Watermelon Salad

**Serving Portions:** 8 | **Preparation Period:** 15 mins.

**Ingredients Required:**

- 2½ lb. seedless watermelon, cubed
- 2 C. strawberries (fresh), slivered
- 2 C. blueberries (fresh)
- 1 C. raspberries (fresh)
- 1 tbsp. ginger root (fresh), grated
- 4 tbsp. mint leaves (fresh), cut up
- 2 tbsp. honey
- ¼ C. lime juice (fresh)

**Procedure of Cooking:**

1. In a large-sized salad bowl, put in watermelon cubes and remnant ingredients and toss it all to mingle nicely.
2. Enjoy immediately.

**Nutritional Facts:**
Calories: 101 | Fat: 0.6g | Carbs: 25.3g | Protein: 1.7g

## Rocket & Orange Salad

**Serving Portions:** 4 | **Preparation Period:** 10 mins.

**Ingredients Required:**

- 3 large-sized oranges, peel, seeds removed and sectioned
- 2 beets, peel removed and slivered
- 6 C. fresh rocket
- ¼ C. walnuts, cut up
- 3 tbsp. olive oil
- 1 pinch of salt

**Procedure of Cooking:**

1. In a salad bowl, put in orange and remnant ingredients and toss it all to mingle nicely.
2. Enjoy immediately.

**Nutritional Facts:**
Calories: 233 | Fat: 15.6g | Carbs: 23.1g | Protein: 4.8g

## Mixed Berries Salad

**Serving Portions:** 8 | **Preparation Period:** 15 mins.

**Ingredients Required:**

- 2 C. strawberries (fresh), hulled and slivered
- 2 C. blueberries (fresh)
- 1½ C. raspberries (fresh)
- ½ C. fresh blackberries
- 1-1¼ tbsp. fresh ginger, grated
- ¼ C. mint leaves (fresh), cut up
- 2 tbsp. honey
- ¼ C. lime juice (fresh)

**Procedure of Cooking:**

1. In a large-sized salad dish, put in watermelon cubes and remnant ingredients and toss it all to mingle nicely
2. Enjoy immediately.

**Nutritional Facts:**
Calories: 74 | Fat: 0.6g | Carbs: 18.1g | Protein: 1.3g

## Mixed Fruit Salad

**Serving Portions:** 4 | **Preparation Period:** 15 mins.

**Ingredients Required:**

- 1 pineapple (fresh), peel removed, cored and cut up
- 2 large-sized mangoes, peel removed, pitted and cut up
- 2 large-sized Fuji apples, cored and cut up
- 2 large-sized pears, cored and cut up
- 2 tsp. ginger root (fresh), finely grated
- 2 tbsp. honey
- ¼ C. lemon juice (fresh)

**Procedure of Cooking:**

1. In a large-sized salad bowl, blend all together the fruits.
2. In a small-sized bowl, put in remnant ingredients and whisk thoroughly.
3. Place honey mixture over fruit mixture and toss it all to mingle nicely.
4. Shift into your refrigerator, covered until chilled thoroughly.

**Nutritional Facts:**
Calories: 161 | Fat: 0.6g | Carbs: 41.6g | Protein: 1.7g

## Mango & Bell Pepper Salad

**Serving Portions:** 6 | **Preparation Period:** 15 mins.

**Ingredients Required:**

**For the Dressing:**

- 1 fresh Serrano pepper, cut up
- 1 tbsp. cilantro (fresh), cut up
- 1 tsp. ginger root (fresh), cut up
- ¼ C. golden raisins, soaked in boiling water for around 30 minutes and drained
- 3 tbsp. extra-virgin olive oil
- 2 tbsp. balsamic vinegar
- Salt, as desired

**For the Salad:**

- 8 C. fresh mixed baby greens
- 2 medium-sized bell peppers, seeds removed and slivered thinly
- 1 large-sized mango, peel removed, pitted and cubed

**Procedure of Cooking:**

1. For the dressing: in a clean mixer, put in Serrano pepper and remnant ingredients and process to form a smooth mixture.
2. Reserve 1 tbsp. of the dressing.
3. In a large-sized bowl, put in greens and remnant dressing and toss it all to mingle nicely.
4. In another bowl, put in bell pepper, mango and reserved dressing and toss it all to mingle nicely.
5. Divide the greens and mango mixture in serving bowls.
6. Enjoy immediately.

**Nutritional Facts:**
Calories: 131 | Fat: 7.4g | Carbs: 17.4g | Protein: 1.6g

## Beet, Carrot & Apple Salad

**Serving Portions:** 6 | **Preparation Period:** 15 mins.

**Ingredients Required:**

**For the Salad:**

- 1¾ C. apple, peel removed, cored and grate
- 1¾ C. beet, peel removed and grated
- 1¾ C. carrots, peel removed and grate

**For the Dressing:**

- 1-1¼ tbsp. fresh ginger, finely grated
- 1 tbsp. honey
- 2-3 tbsp. lime juice
- 2-3 tbsp. extra-virgin olive oil

**Procedure of Cooking:**

1. In a large-sized salad dish, blend all together salad ingredients.
2. In a small-sized basin, put in dressing ingredients and whisk thoroughly
3. Put the dressing over salad mixture and toss it all to mingle nicely
4. Shift in your refrigerator before enjoying.

**Nutritional Facts:**
Calories: 100| Fat: 2.6g| Carbs: 20.1g| Protein: 1.3g

## Tomato & Mozzarella Salad

**Serving Portions:** 8| **Preparation Period:** 15 mins.

**Ingredients Required:**

- 4 C. cherry tomatoes, halved
- 1½ lb. mozzarella cheese, cubed
- ¼ C. basil leaves (fresh), cut up
- ¼ C. olive oil
- 2 tbsp. lemon juice (fresh)
- 1 tsp. oregano (fresh), finely cut up
- 1 tsp. parsley (fresh), finely cut up
- 1-2 tsp. maple syrup
- Salt and powdered black pepper, as desired

**Procedure of Cooking:**

1. In a salad bowl, blend all together tomatoes, mozzarella and basil.
2. In a small-sized bowl, put in oil and remnant ingredients and whisk to incorporate thoroughly.
3. Place dressing over salad and toss it all to mingle nicely.
4. Enjoy immediately.

**Nutritional Facts:**
Calories: 87| Fat: 7.5g| Carbs: 3.9g| Protein: 2.4g

## Collard Greens & Seeds Salad

**Serving Portions:** 4| **Preparation Period:** 15 mins.| **Cooking Period:** 6 minutes

**Ingredients Required:**

- 1½ tsp. ginger root (fresh), finely grated
- 2 tbsp. apple cider vinegar
- 3 tbsp. olive oil
- 1 tsp. sesame oil, toasted
- 3 tsp. honey, divided
- ½ tsp. red pepper flakes, divided
- Salt, as desired
- 1 tbsp. water
- 2 tbsp. raw sunflower seeds
- 1 tbsp. raw sesame seeds
- 1 tbsp. raw pumpkin seeds
- 10 oz. fresh collard greens, ribs removed and thinly slivered

**Procedure of Cooking:**

1. For the Dressing: in a bowl, put in ginger, vinegar, both oils, 1 tsp. of honey, ¼ tsp. red pepper flakes and salt and whisk to incorporate thoroughly. Put it aside.
2. In another bowl, put in remnant honey, remnant red pepper flakes and water and blend to incorporate thoroughly.
3. Heat a medium-sized, anti-sticking wok on burner at around medium heat.
4. Cook all seeds for around 3 minutes, mixing all the time.
5. Blend in the honey mixture.
6. Cook for around 3 minutes, mixing all the time.
7. Shift the seeds mixture onto bakery paper-lined plate and put it aside to cool thoroughly.
8. After cooling, break the seeds mixture into small pieces.
9. In a large-sized salad bowl, put in greens, 2 tsp. of the dressing and a little salt and toss it all to mingle nicely.

10. With your hands, rub the greens for around 30 seconds.
11. Put in remnant dressing and toss it all to mingle nicely.
12. Enjoy with a decoration of seeds pieces.

**Nutritional Facts:**
Calories: 184| Fat: 15.6g| Carbs: 10.5g| Protein: 3.6g

## Carrot & Radish Salad

**Serving Portions:** 4| **Preparation Period:** 15 mins.

**Ingredients Required:**

- 1 bunch kale (fresh), tough ribs removed and slivered thinly
- 1 large-sized clove garlic, finely cut up
- 2 tbsp. lemon juice (fresh)
- 3 tbsp. extra-virgin olive oil, divide
- 2 medium-sized carrots, peel removed and slivered thinly
- 6 radishes, slivered thinly
- 2 tbsp. apple cider vinegar
- 1/3 C. unsweetened coconut flakes, toasted

**Procedure of Cooking:**

1. In a large-sized bowl, put in kale, garlic, lemon juice and 1 tbsp. of olive oil and toss it all to mingle nicely.
2. With your hands, rub the kale.
3. Put in in remnant olive oil and toss it all to mingle nicely.
4. Put it aside for around 15 minutes, stringing time to time.
5. In another bowl, blend all together the carrots, radishes and vinegar.
6. Put it aside for around 15 minutes, mixing time to time.
7. Put in carrot mixture in the bowl with kale mixture and toss to blend.
8. Enjoy with a decoration of coconut flakes.

**Nutritional Facts:**
Calories: 168| Fat: 13.7g| Carbs: 9.4g| Protein: 0.7g

## Lentil & Apple Salad

**Serving Portions:** 6| **Preparation Period:** 15 mins.| **Cooking Period:** 30 mins.

**Ingredients Required:**

**For the Salad:**

- 1 C. French green lentils
- 3granny Smith apples, cored and cut up finely
- ½ C. sunflower seeds, toasted
- ½ C. cilantro (fresh), cut up

**For the Dressing:**

- 1 tsp. ginger root (fresh), grated
- 1 tsp. honey
- ¼ C. lime juice (fresh)
- ¼ C. extra-virgin olive oil
- Salt and powdered black pepper, as desired

**Procedure of Cooking:**

1. In a large-sized saucepan of water, put in lentils on burner at around high heat.
2. Cook the mixture until boiling.
3. Immediately turn the heat at around low.
4. Cook with a cover for around 22-25 minutes.
5. Drain the lentils thoroughly and shift into a large-sized bowl. Put it aside to cool.
6. Put in remnant salad ingredients and blend.
7. In another bowl, put in all dressing ingredients and whisk to incorporate thoroughly.
8. Place dressing over lentil mixture and blend to incorporate thoroughly.
9. Enjoy immediately.

**Nutritional Facts:**
Calories: 271 | Fat: 10.9g | Carbs: 36.7g | Protein: 9.4g

# Quinoa Salad

**Serving Portions:** 4 | **Preparation Period:** 15 mins. | **Cooking Period:** 20 mins.

**Ingredients Required:**

**For the Salad:**

- 2 C. water
- 1 C. quinoa
- Salt, as desired
- 2 C. cherry tomatoes, halved
- 2 C. bell peppers, seeds removed and cut up
- 1 C. black olives, pitted
- ½ C. frozen corn, thawed
- ¼ C. scallion greens, cut up

**For the Dressing:**

- 1 tbsp. ginger root (fresh), finely cut up finely
- 1 tbsp. sesame seeds
- 2 tbsp. sesame oil
- 2 tbsp. apple cider vinegar

**Procedure of Cooking:**

1. In a medium-sized saucepan, put in water, quinoa and salt on burner at around high heat.
2. Cook the mixture until boiling.
3. Immediately turn the heat at around low.
4. Cook with a cover for around 15 minutes.
5. Shift the quinoa into a large-sized bowl.
6. Put in remnant salad ingredients and blend to incorporate.
7. In a separate bowl, put in all dressing ingredients and blend to incorporate thoroughly.
8. Place dressing over quinoa mixture and blend to incorporate thoroughly.

9. Enjoy immediately.

**Nutritional Facts:**
Calories: 328 | Fat: 14.7g | Carbs: 43g | Protein: 8.9g

# Chicken & Fruit Salad

**Serving Portions:** 4 | **Preparation Period:** 15 mins.

**Ingredients Required:**

**For the Vinaigrette:**

- 2 tbsp. apple cider vinegar
- 2 tbsp. extra-virgin olive oil
- Salt and powdered black pepper, as desired

**For the Salad:**

- 2 C. cooked chicken, cubed
- 8 C. lettuce, torn
- 2 apples, peel removed, cored and cut up
- 2 C. strawberries (fresh), slivered
- ¼ C. almonds, cut up

**Procedure of Cooking:**

1. For the vinaigrette: in a small-sized bowl, put in vinegar, oil, salt and pepper and whisk thoroughly.
2. For the salad: in a large-sized salad bowl, cooked chicken and remnant ingredients and blend to incorporate.
3. Place vinaigrette over chicken mixture and toss it all to mingle nicely.
4. Enjoy immediately.

**Nutritional Facts:**
Calories: 298 | Fat: 12.7g | Carbs: 25.6g | Protein: 22.8g

# Chicken, Jicama & Carrot Salad

**Serving Portions:** 4 | **Preparation Period:** 15 mins.

**Ingredients Required:**

**For the Dressing:**

- 1 tbsp. ginger root (fresh), cut up
- 3 tbsp. coconut cream
- 2 tbsp. lime juice (fresh)
- 2 tbsp. sesame oil

**For the Salad:**

- 2 C. cooked chicken, cut up
- 1 C. carrot, peel removed and cut up
- 2 scallions, cut up
- ½ C. jicama, cut up
- ¼ C. cilantro (fresh), cut up
- 1 tbsp. sesame seeds

**Procedure of Cooking:**

1. For the dressing: in a clean mixer, put in ginger and remnant ingredients and blend to incorporate thoroughly.
2. In another large salad bowl, blend all together salad ingredients.
3. Pour dressing over salad and toss it all to mingle nicely.
4. Enjoy immediately.

**Nutritional Facts:**
Calories: 196 | Fat: 8.5g | Carbs: 7.5g | Protein: 21.7g

## Steak & Veggie Salad

**Serving Portions:** 8 | **Preparation Period:** 15 mins. | **Cooking Period:** 16 mins.

**Ingredients Required:**

**For the Steak:**

- 2 cloves garlic, crushed
- 1 tsp. ginger root (fresh), grated
- 1 tbsp. honey
- 2 tbsp. olive oil
- Salt and powdered black pepper, as desired

- 1½ lb. grass-fed flank steak, fat removed

**For the Dressing:**

- 1 clove garlic, finely cut up
- 4 tbsp. extra-virgin olive oil
- 3 tbsp. lime juice (fresh)
- ¼ tsp. red pepper flakes
- Salt and powdered black pepper, as desired

**For the Salad:**

- 3 C. cucumber, slivered
- 3 C. cherry tomatoes, halved
- 4 tbsp. mint leaves (fresh)
- 8 C. spinach (fresh), torn

**Procedure of Cooking:**

1. For the steak: in a large-sized, sealable bag, blend all together garlic and remnant ingredients except for steak.
2. Put in steak and blend with marinade.
3. Seal the bag and shift into your refrigerator to marinate for around 24 hours.
4. Take off from your refrigerator and put it aside for around 15 minutes.
5. Lightly spray a grill pan and heat on burner at around medium-high heat
6. Discard the excess marinade from steak and place in grill pan.
7. Cook for around 6-8 minutes from both sides.
8. Take off the steak from grill pan and place onto a chopping block for around 10 minutes before slicing.
9. For the dressing: in a small-sized bowl, put in garlic and remnant ingredients and whisk thoroughly.
10. For the salad: in a large-sized salad bowl, blend all together cucumber and remnant ingredients.
11. Divide into serving portions.
12. Divide salad onto serving plates and top with steak slices.
13. Drizzle with dressing and enjoy immediately.

**Nutritional Facts:**
Calories: 298 | Fat: 17.9g | Carbs: 9.4g | Protein: 25.7g

## Salmon, Orange & Beet Salad

**Serving Portions:** 4 | **Preparation Period:** 15 mins.

**Ingredients Required:**

**For the Salad:**

- 12 oz. cooked salmon, cut up
- 4 large-sized oranges, peel, seeds removed and roughly cut up
- 1 C. cooked beets, peel removed and cut up
- ½ of avocado, peel removed, pitted and cut up
- 1 small-sized red onion, cut up
- 4 C. lettuce, torn
- ¼ C. pistachios, cut up

**For the Dressing:**

- 1 tsp. fresh orange zest, finely grated
- 4 tbsp. orange juice (fresh)
- 2 tbsp. extra-virgin olive oil
- 3 tsp. balsamic vinegar
- 1 tsp. Dijon mustard
- ¼-½ tsp. red chili powder
- Salt and powdered black pepper, as desired

**Procedure of Cooking:**

1. In a large-sized bowl, blend all together all salad ingredients.
2. In another bowl, put in all dressing ingredients and blend to incorporate thoroughly.
3. Place dressing over quinoa mixture and blend to incorporate thoroughly.
4. Enjoy immediately.

**Nutritional Facts:**
Calories: 299 | Fat: 15.8g | Carbs: 23.4g | Protein: 20g

## Salmon & Veggie Salad

**Serving Portions:** 2 | **Preparation Period:** 15 mins.

**Ingredients Required:**

- 6 oz. cooked wild salmon, cut up
- 1 C. cucumber, slivered
- 1 C. red bell pepper, seeds removed and slivered
- ½ C. grape tomatoes, quartered
- 1 tbsp. scallion green, cut up
- 1 C. lettuce, torn
- 1 C. spinach (fresh), torn
- 2 tbsp. olive oil
- 2 tbsp. lemon juice (fresh)

**Procedure of Cooking:**

1. In a salad bowl, put in salmon and remnant ingredients and toss it all to mingle nicely.
2. Enjoy immediately.

**Nutritional Facts:**
Calories: 279 | Fat: 19.8g | Carbs: 10.1g | Protein: 18.6g

## Tuna & Egg Salad

**Serving Portions:** 4 | **Preparation Period:** 15 mins.

**Ingredients Required:**

**For the Dressing:**

- 2 tbsp. fresh dill, finely cut up
- 2 tbsp. olive oil
- 1 tbsp. lime juice (fresh)
- Salt and powdered black pepper, as desired

**For the Salad:**

- 4 C. spinach (fresh), torn
- 2 (6-oz.) cans water-packed tuna, drained and flaked
- 6 hard-boiled eggs, peel removed and slivered
- 1 C. tomato, cut up
- 1 large-sized cucumber, slivered

**Procedure of Cooking:**

1. For the dressing: place dill, oil, lime juice, salt and black pepper in a small-sized bowl and whisk to incorporate thoroughly.
2. Divide the spinach onto serving plates and top each with tuna, egg, cucumber and tomato.
3. Drizzle with dressing and enjoy.

**Nutritional Values**
Calories: 274 | Fat: 14.7g | Carbs: 7g | Protein: 29.8g

## Shrimp & Greens Salad

**Serving Portions:** 6 | **Preparation Period:** 15 mins. | **Cooking Period:** 6 minutes

**Ingredients Required:**

- 1 tbsp. olive oil
- 1 clove garlic, crushed and divided
- 2 tbsp. rosemary (fresh), cut up
- 1 lb. shrimp, peeled and deveined
- Salt and powdered black pepper, as desired
- 4 C. arugula (fresh)
- 2 C. lettuce, torn
- 2 tbsp. olive oil
- 2 tbsp. lime juice (fresh)

**Procedure of Cooking:**

1. In a large-sized wok, sizzle the oil on burner at around medium heat.
2. Cook 1 clove garlic for around 1 minute.

3. Put in shrimp with salt and pepper and blend.
4. Cook for around 4-5 minutes.
5. Take off from burner and put it aside to cool.
6. In a large-sized bowl, put in shrimp, arugula, oil, lime juice, salt and pepper and toss it all to mingle nicely.
7. Enjoy immediately.

**Nutritional Facts:**
Calories: 157 | Fat: 8.2g | Carbs: 3.1g | Protein: 17.7g

## Shrimp & Tomato Salad

**Serving Portions:** 4 | **Preparation Period:** 20 mins. | **Cooking Period:** 5 minutes

**Ingredients Required:**

**For the Shrimp:**

- 1 tbsp. olive oil
- ¾ lb. shrimp, peeled and deveined
- 2 cloves garlic, finely cut up
- Salt, as desired
- 1 tbsp. lemon juice (fresh)

**For the Salad:**

- 4 C. lettuce, torn
- 1 C. frozen corn, thawed
- 2 large-sized tomatoes, cut up
- 1 C. onion, slivered
- 2 tbsp. olive oil
- Salt and powdered black pepper, as desired

**Procedure of Cooking:**

1. In a medium-sized wok, sizzle olive oil on burner at around medium-high heat.
2. Cook the shrimp for around 2 minutes.
3. Flip the shrimp and immediately turn the heat at around medium-low.
4. Blend in the garlic and salt.
5. Cook for around 2-3 minutes.

6. Blend in lemon juice and take off from burner.
7. Put it aside to cool thoroughly.
8. In a large-sized salad bowl, put in shrimp and all salad ingredients and toss it all to mingle nicely.
9. Enjoy immediately.

**Nutritional Facts:**
Calories: 263| Fat: 12.7g| Carbs: 17g| Protein: 22.1g

## Scallops Salad

**Serving Portions:** 6| **Preparation Period:** 20 mins.| **Cooking Period:** 5 minutes

**Ingredients Required:**

**For the Scallops:**

- 2 tbsp. olive oil
- 1½ lb. sea scallops
- Salt and powdered black pepper, as desired

**For the Dressing:**

- 2-3 tbsp. plain Greek yogurt
- 3 tbsp. Dijon mustard
- Salt and powdered black pepper, as desired

**For the Salad:**

- 6 hard-boiled eggs, peel removed and slivered
- 3 medium-sized apples, cored and slivered
- 2 C. purple cabbage, cut up
- 1/3 C. feta cheese, crumbled

**Procedure of Cooking:**

1. In a large-sized anti-sticking wok, sizzle the olive oil on burner at around medium-high heat.
2. Blend in the scallops, salt and pepper and immediately turn the heat at around high.
3. Cook for around 5 minutes, flipping once halfway through.
4. Shift the scallops into a bowl and put it aside to cool.
5. For the dressing: in a bowl, put in yogurt and remnant ingredients and whisk to incorporate thoroughly.
6. For the salad: in a large-sized serving bowl, put in the eggs and remnant ingredients and mix.
7. Top with scallops and drizzle with dressing.
8. Enjoy immediately.

**Nutritional Facts:**
Calories: 297| Fat: 12.3g| Carbs: 20.9g| Protein: 27g

# Soup & Stews Recipes

## Chicken & Tomato Soup

**Serving Portions:** 4 | **Preparation Period:** 15 mins. | **Cooking Period:** 23 mins.

**Ingredients Required:**

- 4 C. homemade chicken broth
- 2 large-sized tomatoes, peel, seeds removed and cut up
- 1 jalapeño pepper, seeds removed and finely cut up
- 1 clove garlic, finely cut up
- 1 tsp. ginger root (fresh), finely cut up
- ½ tsp. powdered cumin
- 2 C. cooked chicken, shredded
- 3 scallions, finely cut up
- Salt, as desired
- ¼ C. cilantro (fresh), cut up
- 2 tbsp. lime juice (fresh)

**Procedure of Cooking:**

1. In a large-sized soup pan, put in broth on burner at around medium heat.
2. Cook the broth until boiling.
3. Put in tomatoes, jalapeño pepper, garlic, ginger and cumin.
4. Cook for around 15 minutes.
5. Put in chicken, scallion and salt and blend to incorporate.
6. Immediately turn the heat at around low.
7. Cook for around 1-2 minutes.
8. Blend in the cilantro and lime juice and take off the soup pan from burner.
9. Enjoy immediately.

**Nutritional Facts:**
Calories: 166 | Fat: 2.4g | Carbs: 5.4g | Protein: 30.5g

## Chicken & Veggie Soup

**Serving Portions:** 8 | **Preparation Period:** 15 mins. | **Cooking Period:** 40 mins.

**Ingredients Required:**

- 1½ tbsp. olive oil
- 2 large-sized onion, cut up
- 2 large-sized sweet potato, peel removed and cut up
- 3 zucchinis, cut up
- 1 C. fresh green peas, shelled
- 4 (6-oz.) boneless chicken breasts
- 2 tsp. powdered cumin
- 1 tbsp. powdered turmeric
- 4 C. homemade chicken broth
- 6 C. water
- ½ C. cilantro (fresh), cut up

**Procedure of Cooking:**

1. In a large-sized soup pan, sizzle the oil on burner at around medium heat.
2. Cook the onion for around 3-5 minutes, stirring all the time.
3. Blend in vegetables.
4. Cook for around 5 minutes.
5. Blend in remnant ingredients.
6. Cook the mixture until boiling.
7. Immediately turn the heat at around medium-low.
8. Cook with a cover for around 10-15 minutes
9. With a frying ladle, take off the chicken breasts from soup and place into a bowl.
10. With two forks, shred the chicken breasts.
11. Return the shredded chicken into the soup.
12. Cook for around 10 minutes.
13. Enjoy hot with the decoration of cilantro.

**Nutritional Facts:**

Calories: 279 | Fat: 10.1g | Carbs: 16.4g | Protein: 30.1g

## Turkey & Veggies Soup

**Serving Portions:** 8 | **Preparation Period:** 15 mins. | **Cooking Period:** 20 mins.

**Ingredients Required:**

- 8 C. homemade chicken broth
- 2-3 C. broccoli, cut up
- 8 oz. mushrooms (fresh), slivered
- 6 scallions, cut up
- 1 (1-inch) piece ginger root (fresh), finely cut up
- 4 cloves garlic, finely cut up
- 1½ lb. cooked turkey meat, thinly slivered
- ½ tsp. powdered cumin
- ½ tsp. powdered turmeric
- ½ tsp. red pepper flakes
- 2 tbsp. lime juice (fresh)

**Procedure of Cooking:**

1. In a large-sized soup pan, put in broth on burner at around high heat.
2. Cook the broth until boiling.
3. Blend in broccoli pieces.
4. Cook for around 1-2 minutes.
5. Blend in mushroom, scallions, ginger and garlic.
6. Cook for around 7-8 minutes.
7. Blend in turkey meat, spices and lime juice and immediately turn the heat at around low.
8. Cook for around 3-5 minutes.
9. Enjoy hot.

**Nutritional Facts:**
Calories: 203 | Fat: 5.8g | Carbs: 4.6g | Protein: 31.6g

## Ground Turkey & Cabbage Soup

**Serving Portions:** 8 | **Preparation Period:** 15 mins. | **Cooking Period:** 45 mins.

**Ingredients Required:**

- 1 tbsp. olive oil
- 1 large-sized onion, cut up
- 1 lb. lean ground turkey
- 2 cloves garlic, finely cut up
- 1 tbsp. ginger root (fresh), finely cut up
- 1 tsp. salt
- ½ tsp. powdered black pepper
- 6 C. cabbage, shredded
- 2½ C. tomatoes, cut up finely
- ½ tsp. thyme (dried)
- ½ tsp. oregano (dried)
- 1 bay leaf
- ½ tsp. paprika
- ½ tsp. powdered cumin
- ½ tsp. powdered cinnamon
- 6 C. homemade chicken broth

**Procedure of Cooking:**

1. In a large-sized soup pan, sizzle the oil on burner at around medium-high heat.
2. Cook the onion for around 3-5 minutes.
3. Put in ground turkey, garlic, ginger, salt and pepper and blend to incorporate.
4. Immediately turn the heat at around medium-high.
5. Cook for around 7-8 minutes.
6. Put in cabbage, tomatoes, herbs, bay leaf, spices and broth.
7. Cook the mixture until boiling.
8. Immediately turn the heat at around low.
9. Cook for around 25 minutes.
10. Season with more salt and pepper and enjoy hot.

**Nutritional Facts:**
Calories: 210 | Fat: 6.7g | Carbs: 10.8g | Protein: 26.6g

## Beef & Lentil Soup

**Serving Portions:** 8 | **Preparation Period:** 15 mins. | **Cooking Period:** 2 hrs.

**Ingredients Required:**

- 2 tbsp. olive oil
- 1 lb. grass-fed beef chuck, fat removed and cut into cubes
- Salt and powdered black pepper, as desired
- 1 large-sized carrot, peel removed and cut up
- 1 large-sized celery stalk, cut up
- 2 large-sized onions, cut up
- 6 cloves garlic, cut up
- 1 tsp. rosemary (dried)
- 1 tsp. oregano (dried)
- 3 large-sized sweet potato, peel removed and cut up
- 4 C. homemade chicken broth
- 4-5 C. water
- 4-5 C. tomatoes, cut up
- 2 C. dry lentils, rinsed
- ¼ C. parsley (fresh), cut up

**Procedure of Cooking:**

1. Rub the beef cubes with salt and pepper.
2. In a large-sized soup pan, sizzle the olive oil on burner at around medium-high heat.
3. Cook the beef cubes for around 8 minutes.
4. With a frying ladle, shift the beef into a bowl and put it aside.
5. In the same pan, put in carrot, celery onion, garlic and dried herbs on burner at around medium heat.
6. Cook for around 5 minutes.
7. Put in sweet potatoes.
8. Cook for around 4–5 minutes.
9. Put in cooked beef, tomatoes, broth and water and immediately turn the heat at around high.
10. Cook the mixture until boiling.
11. Immediately turn the heat at around low.
12. Cook with a cover for around 1 hour.
13. Put in lentils.
14. Cook with a cover for around 40 minutes.
15. Blend in black pepper and take off from burner.
16. Enjoy hot with the decoration of parsley.

**Nutritional Facts:**
Calories: 298 | Fat: 8.3g | Carbs: 29.9g | Protein: 26.6g

## Salmon & Cabbage Soup

**Serving Portions:** 4 | **Preparation Period:** 15 mins. | **Cooking Period:** 30 mins.

**Ingredients Required:**

- 2 tbsp. olive oil
- 1 shallot, cut up
- 2 cloves garlic, finely cut up
- 1 tbsp. ginger root (fresh), finely cut up
- 1 jalapeño pepper, cut up
- 1 large-sized cabbage head, cut up
- 4 C. homemade vegetable broth
- 3 (4-oz.) boneless salmon fillets, cubed
- ¼ C. cilantro (fresh), finely cut up
- 2 tbsp. lemon juice (fresh)
- Salt and powdered black pepper, as desired
- 3 tbsp. parsley (fresh), cut up

**Procedure of Cooking:**

1. In a large-sized soup pan, sizzle the oil on burner at around medium heat.
2. Cook the shallot and garlic for 2-3 minutes.
3. Put in cabbage and sauté for around 3-4 minutes.
4. Put in broth and immediately turn the heat at around high.
5. Cook the mixture until boiling

6. Immediately turn the heat at around medium-low.
7. Cook for around 10 minutes.
8. Put in salmon.
9. Cook for around 5-6 minutes.
10. Blend in the cilantro, lemon juice, salt and pepper.
11. Cook for around 1-2 minutes.
12. Enjoy hot with the decoration of dill.

**Nutritional Facts:**
Calories: 260 | Fat: 12.7g | Carbs: 21g | Protein: 19.9g

## Shrimp & Mushroom Soup

**Serving Portions:** 6 | **Preparation Period:** 15 mins. | **Cooking Period:** 30 mins.

**Ingredients Required:**

- 1 tbsp. olive oil
- 1 small-sized onion, cut up
- 1 tbsp. lemongrass, finely cut up
- 1 tbsp. ginger root (fresh), finely cut up
- 2 cloves garlic, finely cut up
- 1 tbsp. red curry paste
- 3 C. homemade chicken broth
- 2 (14-oz.) cans coconut milk (unsweetened)
- 8 oz. shiitake mushrooms (fresh), slivered
- 1 lb. medium shrimp, peeled and deveined
- 1½ tbsp. lime juice (fresh)
- 2 tsp. lime zest, grated
- Salt, as desired

**Procedure of Cooking:**

1. In a large-sized soup pan, sizzle the oil on burner at around medium heat.
2. Cook the onion for around 5-7 minutes.
3. Blend in the lemongrass, ginger, garlic and curry paste and sauté for around 1 minute.
4. Blend in the broth.

5. Cook for around 10 minutes.
6. Put in coconut milk and blend to incorporate.
7. Put in in the mushrooms.
8. Cook for around 5 minutes.
9. Put in shrimp.
10. Cook for around 5 minutes.
11. Blend in the lime juice, zest and salt and enjoy hot.

**Nutritional Facts:**
Calories: 404 | Fat: 29.7g | Carbs: 9.8g | Protein: 23.8g

## Lentil & Kale Soup

**Serving Portions:** 8 | **Preparation Period:** 15 mins. | **Cooking Period:** 1¼ hrs.

**Ingredients Required:**

- 2 tbsp. olive oil
- 2 carrots, peel removed and cut up
- 2 celery stalks, cut up
- 2 sweet onions, cut up
- 3 cloves garlic, finely cut up
- 1¾ C. brown lentils, rinsed
- 2½ C. tomatoes, finely cut up
- ¼ tsp. basil (dried)
- ¼ tsp. oregano (dried)
- ¼ tsp. thyme (dried)
- 1 tsp. powdered cumin
- ½ tsp. powdered coriander
- ½ tsp. paprika
- 6 C. homemade vegetable broth
- 3 C. spinach (fresh), cut up
- Sea salt and powdered black pepper, as desired
- 2 tbsp. lemon juice (fresh)

**Procedure of Cooking:**

1. In a large-sized soup pan, sizzle the oil on burner at around medium heat.
2. Cook the carrot, celery and onion for 5 minutes.

3. Put in garlic and sauté for around 1 minute.
4. Put in lentils and sauté for around 3 minutes.
5. Blend in the tomatoes, herbs, spices.
6. Cook the mixture until boiling.
7. Immediately turn the heat at around low.
8. Cook with a cover for around 1 hour.
9. Blend in the kale, salt and pepper.
10. Cook for around 4-5 minutes.
11. Blend in the lemon juice and enjoy hot.

**Nutritional Facts:**
Calories: 275 | Fat: 6.1g | Carbs: 39.7g | Protein: 18.1g

## Broccoli Soup

**Serving Portions:** 4 | **Preparation Period:** 15 mins. | **Cooking Period:** 45 mins.

**Ingredients Required:**

- 1 tbsp. coconut oil
- 1 celery stalk, cut up
- ½ C. onion, cut up
- Salt, as desired
- 1 tsp. powdered turmeric
- 2 cloves garlic, finely cut up
- 1 large-sized head broccoli, cut into florets
- ¼ tsp. ginger root (fresh), grated
- 1 bay leaf
- 1/8 tsp. powdered cayenne pepper
- Powdered black pepper, as desired
- 5 C. homemade vegetable broth
- 1 small-sized avocado, peel removed, pitted and cut up
- 1 tbsp. lemon juice (fresh)

**Procedure of Cooking:**

1. In a large-sized soup pan, sizzle the oil on burner at around medium heat.
2. Cook the celery, onion and some salt for around 3-4 minutes.

3. Put in turmeric and garlic and sauté for around 1 minute.
4. Put in salt and remnant ingredients except for avocado and lemon juice. Cook until boiling
5. Immediately turn the heat at around medium-low.
6. Cook with a cover for around 25-30 minutes.
7. Take off the pan of soup from burner and discard the bay leaf.
8. Put it aside to cool slightly.
9. In a clean mixer, put in soup and avocado in batches and process to form a smooth mixture.
10. Return the soup into the same pan on burner at around medium heat.
11. Cook for around 3-5 minutes.
12. Enjoy immediately with the drizzling of lemon juice.

**Nutritional Facts:**
Calories: 169 | Fat: 11g | Carbs: 10.4g | Protein: 8.8g

## Asparagus Soup

**Serving Portions:** 4 | **Preparation Period:** 15 mins. | **Cooking Period:** 40 mins.

**Ingredients Required:**

- 1 tbsp. olive oil
- 3 scallions, cut up
- 1½ lb. fresh asparagus, cut up
- 4 C. homemade vegetable broth
- 2 tbsp. lemon juice (fresh)
- Sea salt and powdered black pepper, as desired
- 2 tbsp. coconut cream

**Procedure of Cooking:**

1. In a large-sized pan, sizzle the oil on burner at around medium heat.
2. Cook the scallion for around 4-5 minutes.
3. Blend in the asparagus and broth.
4. Cook the mixture until boiling.

5. Immediately turn the heat at around low.
6. Cook with a cover for 25-30 minutes.
7. Take off from burner and put it aside to cool slightly.
8. Now, Shift the soup into a high-power mixer in 2 batches and process to form a smooth mixture.
9. Return the soup into the same pan on burner at around medium heat.
10. Cook for 4-5 minutes.
11. Blend in the lemon juice, salt and black pepper and take off from burner.
12. Enjoy hot with a topping of coconut cream.

**Nutritional Facts:**

Calories: 125 | Fat: 6.9g | Carbs: 8.9g | Protein: 9g

## Chicken & Tomato Stew

**Serving Portions:** 8 | **Preparation Period:** 15 mins. | **Cooking Period:** 30 mins.

**Ingredients Required:**

- 2 tbsp. olive oil
- 1 onion, cut up
- ½ tbsp. ginger root (fresh), finely grated
- 1 tbsp. garlic, finely cut up
- 1 tsp. powdered turmeric
- 1 tsp. powdered cumin
- 1 tsp. powdered coriander
- 1 tsp. paprika
- 1 tsp. powdered cayenne pepper
- 5 (6-oz.) boneless chicken thighs, cut into 1-inch pieces
- 3 Roma tomatoes, cut up
- 1 (14-oz.) can coconut milk (unsweetened)
- Salt and powdered black pepper, as desired
- 1/3 C. cilantro (fresh), cut up

**Procedure of Cooking:**

1. In a large-sized saucepan, sizzle the oil on burner at around medium heat.
2. Cook the onion for around 8-10 minutes.
3. Put in ginger, garlic and spices and sauté for around 1 minute.
4. Put in chicken.
5. Cook for around 4-5 minutes.
6. Blend in tomatoes, coconut milk, salt and pepper.
7. Cook the mixture until boiling.
8. Immediately turn the heat at around low.
9. Cook with a cover for around 10-15 minutes.
10. Blend in cilantro and enjoy hot.

**Nutritional Facts:**
Calories: 245 | Fat: 14.8g | Carbs: 5.1g | Protein: 22.1g

## Chicken & Spinach Stew

**Serving Portions:** 8 | **Preparation Period:** 15 mins. | **Cooking Period:** 30 mins.

**Ingredients Required:**

- 2 tbsp. olive oil
- 1 medium-sized onion, cut up
- 1 tbsp. garlic, finely cut up
- 1 tbsp. ginger root (fresh), finely cut up
- 1 tsp. powdered turmeric
- 1 tsp. powdered cumin
- 1 tsp. powdered coriander
- 1 tsp. paprika
- 1 tsp. powdered cayenne pepper
- 6 (4-oz.) boneless chicken thighs, cut into pieces
- 4 tomatoes, cut up
- 1 (14-oz.) can coconut milk (unsweetened)
- Salt and powdered black pepper, as desired
- 3 C. spinach (fresh), cut up

**Procedure of Cooking:**

1. Sizzle oil in a large-sized, heavy-bottomed saucepan on burner at around medium heat.
2. Cook the onion for around 3-4 minutes.
3. Put in ginger, garlic and spices and sauté for around 1 minute.
4. Put in chicken and blend.
5. Cook for around 4-5 minutes.
6. Put in tomatoes, coconut milk, salt and black pepper.
7. Cook the mixture until boiling.
8. Immediately turn the heat at around low.
9. Cook with a cover for around 10-15 minutes.
10. Blend in the spinach.
11. Cook for around 4-5 minutes.
12. Enjoy hot.

**Nutritional Facts:**
Calories: 231| Fat: 13.1g | Carbs: 6.3g | Protein: 20.9g

## Chicken & Veggie Stew

**Serving Portions:** 6| **Preparation Period:** 15 mins.| **Cooking Period:** 30 mins.

**Ingredients Required:**

- 3 tbsp. olive oi
- ½ C. onion, cut up
- ¾ C. bell pepper, seeds removed and cut up
- 3¾ C. chicken broth
- 1 bay leaf
- 2/3 C. whipping cream
- 12 oz. asparagus, cut into 2-inch pieces
- 8 oz. mushrooms (fresh), slivered
- 1 C. green beans (fresh), cut into 2-inch pieces
- 2½ lb. cooked boneless chicken, cut up
- Salt and powdered black pepper, as desired
- 2 tbsp. thyme (fresh), finely cut up

**Procedure of Cooking:**

1. In a large-sized Dutch oven, sizzle the oil on burner at around medium heat.
2. Cook the onion and bell pepper for around 4-5 minutes.
3. Put in broth and bay leaf.
4. Cook the mixture until boiling.
5. Cook for around 10 minutes.
6. Meanwhile, in a small-sized pan, put in cream on burner at around medium heat.
7. Cook for around 5-7 minutes, mixing time to time.
8. Put in asparagus, mushrooms and green beans into the pan of broth mixture.
9. Cook for around 7-10 minutes.
10. Put in cooked chicken and blend to incorporate.
11. Immediately turn the heat at around low.
12. Cook for around 3-5 minutes.
13. Blend in the salt, pepper and thyme and immediately take off from burner.
14. Enjoy hot.

**Nutritional Facts:**
Calories: 464| Fat: 17.8g | Carbs: 9g | Protein: 64.9g

## Beef & Tomato Stew

**Serving Portions:** 8| **Preparation Period:** 15 mins.| **Cooking Period:** 1 hr. 5 mins.

**Ingredients Required:**

- 2 lb. grass-fed beef top sirloin, cut into cubes
- Salt, as desired
- 1 tbsp. olive oil
- 1 large-sized onion, slivered
- 4 jalapeño peppers, stemmed and slivered
- 1 tsp. oregano (dried)
- 1 tsp. powdered cumin
- 2½ C. tomatoes, finely cut up
- 1 onion, cut into rings
- ¼ C. cilantro, cut up

**Procedure of Cooking:**

1. In a large-sized bowl, put in beef cubes and salt and toss it all to mingle nicely.
2. Put it aside at room temperature for around 1 hour.
3. In a large-sized Dutch oven, sizzle the olive oil on burner at around high heat.
4. Sear the beef cubes for around 4-5 minutes.
5. Put in slivered onion, jalapeño pepper, oregano and cumin.
6. Cook for around 10 minutes, mixing time to time.
7. Put in in the tomatoes and blend.
8. Cook the mixture until boiling.
9. Immediately turn the heat at around low.
10. Cook with a cover for around 45 minutes, mixing time to time.
11. Top with onion rings and cilantro and enjoy hot.

**Nutritional Facts:**
Calories: 264| Fat: 10.2g| Carbs: 6g| Protein: 35.4g

## Beef & Carrot Stew

**Serving Portions:** 6| **Preparation Period:** 15 mins.| **Cooking Period:** 55 minutes

**Ingredients Required:**

- 1½ lb. grass-fed beef stew meat, fat removed and cut up
- Salt and powdered black pepper, as desired
- 1 tbsp. olive oil
- 1 C. homemade tomato puree
- 4 C. homemade chicken broth
- 3 carrots, peel removed and slivered
- 2 cloves garlic, finely cut up
- ½ tbsp. thyme (dried)
- 1 tsp. parsley (dried)
- 1 tsp. rosemary (dried)
- 1 tbsp. paprika
- 1 tsp. onion powder

- 1 tsp. garlic powder
- 3 tbsp. parsley (fresh), cut up

**Procedure of Cooking:**

1. In a large-sized bowl, put in beef cubes, salt and pepper and toss it all to mingle nicely.
2. In a Dutch oven, sizzle the oil on burner at around medium-high heat.
3. Cook the beef cubes for around 4-5 minutes.
4. Put in in remnant ingredients and blend to incorporate.
5. Immediately turn the heat at around high.
6. Cook the mixture until boiling.
7. Immediately turn the heat at around low.
8. Cook with a cover for around 40-50 minutes.
9. Blend in the salt and pepper and take off from burner.
10. Enjoy hot.

**Nutritional Facts:**
Calories: 295| Fat: 10.5g| Carbs: 8g| Protein: 39g

## Salmon & Shrimp Stew

**Serving Portions:** 6| **Preparation Period:** 20 mins.| **Cooking Period:** 25 minutes

**Ingredients Required:**

- 2 tbsp. coconut oil
- ½ C. onion, cut up finely
- 2 cloves garlic, finely cut up
- 1 Serrano pepper, cut up
- 1 tsp. smoked paprika
- 4 C. tomatoes, cut up
- 4 C. homemade chicken broth
- 1 lb. salmon fillets, cubed
- 1 lb. shrimp, peeled and deveined
- 2 tbsp. lime juice (fresh)
- Salt and powdered black pepper, as desired

- 3 tbsp. parsley (fresh), cut up

**Procedure of Cooking:**

1. In a large-sized soup pan, sizzle coconut oil on burner at around medium-high heat.
2. Cook the onion for around 5-6 minutes.
3. Put in garlic, Serrano pepper and paprika and sauté for around 1 minute.
4. Put in tomatoes and broth.
5. Cook the mixture until boiling.
6. Immediately turn the heat at around medium.
7. Cook for around 5 minutes.
8. Put in salmon.
9. Cook for around 3-4 minutes.
10. Blend in the shrimp.
11. Cook for around 4-5 minutes.
12. Blend in lemon juice, salt and black pepper and take off from burner.
13. Enjoy hot with the decoration of parsley.

**Nutritional Facts:**
Calories: 247 | Fat: 10.7g | Carbs: 5.1g | Protein: 32.7g

---

## Mushroom& Kale Stew

**Serving Portions:** 8 | **Preparation Period:** 15 mins. | **Cooking Period:** 2 hrs. 20 mins.

**Ingredients Required:**

- 2 tbsp. olive oil
- 1 medium-sized onions, cut up
- 2 C. celery, cut up
- ½ tsp. garlic, finely cut up
- 3 C. kale (fresh), tough ends removed and cut up
- ½ C. fresh mushroom, slivered
- 2½ C. tomatoes, finely cut up
- 1 tsp. rosemary (dried)
- 1 tsp. sage (dried)
- 1 tsp. oregano (dried)
- Salt and powdered black pepper, as desired

- 2 C. homemade vegetable broth
- 4 C. water

**Procedure of Cooking:**

1. In a large-sized saucepan, sizzle olive oil in on burner at around medium heat.
2. Cook the onion, celery and garlic for around 5 minutes.
3. Put in remnant ingredients and blend to incorporate.
4. Immediately turn the heat at around high.
5. Cook the mixture until boiling.
6. Cook for around 10 minutes.
7. Immediately turn the heat at around medium.
8. Cook with a cover for around 15 minutes.
9. Uncover the pan and blend the mixture.
10. Cook for around 15 more minutes, mixing time to time.
11. Immediately turn the heat at around low.
12. Cook with a cover for around 1½ hours.
13. Enjoy hot.

**Nutritional Facts:**
Calories: 77 | Fat: 3.9g | Carbs: 8.4g | Protein: 3g

---

## Mixed Veggie Stew

**Serving Portions:** 4 | **Preparation Period:** 20 mins. | **Cooking Period:** 1 hr.

**Ingredients Required:**

- 2 tbsp. olive oil
- 1¼ C. onion, cut up
- 1 tbsp. garlic, finely cut up
- 1 tbsp. chile paste
- 1½ tbsp. fresh turmeric, grated
- 1½ tsp. powdered cumin
- 1 tsp. powdered cinnamon

- 1 C. carrots, peel removed and roughly cut up
- 1 C. cauliflower, roughly cut up
- 2 C. broccoli, roughly cut up
- 2 C. green cabbage, roughly cut up
- 1 C. coconut water
- 2 C. tomatoes, crushed
- ¾ C. frozen green peas, thawed
- Salt and powdered black pepper, as desired

## Procedure of Cooking:

1. In a large-sized soup pan, sizzle the oil on burner at around medium heat.
2. Cook the onion and garlic for around 10 minutes, mixing time to time.
3. Put in chile paste, turmeric, cumin and cinnamon and sauté for around 1 minute.
4. Blend in carrots.
5. Cook for around 3-4 minutes.
6. Blend in cauliflower and broccoli.
7. Cook for around 2-3 minutes.
8. Blend in cabbage and immediately turn the heat at around low.
9. Cook for around 4-6 minutes.
10. Put in coconut water and tomatoes and blend to incorporate.
11. Immediately turn the heat at around high.
12. Cook the mixture until boiling.
13. Immediately turn the heat at around low.
14. Cook with a cover for around 30 minutes.
15. Blend in green peas, salt and pepper.
16. Cook for around 3-5 minutes.
17. Enjoy hot.

## Nutritional Facts:
Calories: 216 | Fat: 7.9g | Carbs: 31.8g | Protein: 8.2g

## Lentil, Quinoa & Kale Stew

**Serving Portions:** 6 | **Preparation Period:** 15 mins. | **Cooking Period:** 30 mins.

## Ingredients Required:

- 1 tbsp. extra-virgin olive oil
- 3 carrots, peel removed and cut up
- 3 celery stalks, cut up
- 1 onion, cut up
- 4 cloves garlic, finely cut up
- 4 C. tomatoes, cut up
- 1 C. red lentils, rinsed and drained
- ½ C. dried quinoa, rinsed and drained
- 1½ tsp. powdered cumin
- 1 tsp. red chili powder
- 5 C. homemade vegetable broth
- 3 C. kale (fresh), tough ribs removed and cut up
- Salt and powdered black pepper, as desired

## Procedure of Cooking:

1. In a large-sized pan, sizzle the oil on burner at around medium heat.
2. Cook the celery, onion and carrot for around 4-5 minutes.
3. Put in garlic and sauté for around 1 minute.
4. Put in remnant ingredients except the spinach.
5. Cook the mixture until boiling.
6. Immediately turn the heat at around low.
7. Cook with a cover for around 20 minutes.
8. Blend in spinach.
9. Cook for around 3-4 minutes.
10. Blend in the salt and pepper and take off from burner.
11. Enjoy hot.

## Nutritional Facts:
Calories: 283 | Fat: 5.1g | Carbs: 43.3g | Protein: 17.1g

## Quinoa & Veggie Stew

**Serving Portions:** 4
| **Preparation Period:** 15 mins.
| **Cooking Period:** 1 hr.

## Ingredients Required:

- 2 tbsp. olive oil
- 1 large-sized onion, cut up
- Sea salt, as desired
- 2 C. carrot, peel removed and cubed
- 3 cloves garlic, finely cut up
- 1 tsp. powdered cumin
- 1 tsp. powdered cayenne pepper
- 2½ C. plum tomatoes, cut up finely
- ½ C. dry quinoa, rinsed
- 3 C. water
- 3 C. kale (fresh), tough ribs removed and cut up
- 1 tbsp. lime juice (fresh)

## Procedure of Cooking:

1. In a soup pan, sizzle the olive oil on burner at around medium heat.
2. Cook the onion with few pinches of salt for around 4–5 minutes, mixing time to time.
3. Put in carrot.
4. Cook for around 3-4 minutes.
5. Blend in the garlic and spices.
6. Cook for around 1 minute.
7. Blend in the tomatoes, quinoa and water.
8. Cook the mixture until boiling.
9. Immediately turn the heat at around low.
10. Cook with a cover for around 35 minutes.
11. Blend in the kale.
12. Cook for around 10 minutes.
13. Enjoy hot.

## Nutritional Facts:
Calories: 230 | Fat: 8.8g | Carbs: 33.9g | Protein: 6.9g

# Poultry Recipes

## Chicken & Strawberry Lettuce Wraps

**Serving Portions:** 2 | **Preparation Period:** 15 mins.

**Ingredients Required:**

- 4 oz. cooked chicken, cut into strips
- ½ C. strawberries (fresh), hulled and thinly slivered
- 1 small-sized cucumber, thinly slivered
- 1 tbsp. fresh mint leaves, cut up
- 4 large-sized lettuce leaves

**Procedure of Cooking:**

1. In a large-sized bowl, put in chicken and remnant ingredients except for lettuce leaves and toss it all to mingle nicely.
2. Place the lettuce leaves onto serving plates.
3. Divide the chicken mixture over each leaf.
4. Enjoy immediately.

**Nutritional Facts:**
Calories: 244 | Fat: 4g | Carbs: 17g | Protein: 35.4g

## Chicken Pita Sandwiches

**Serving Portions:** 4 | **Preparation Period:** 20 mins. | **Cooking Period:** 8 mins.

**Ingredients Required:**

**For the Chicken Marinade:**

- 2 tbsp. lemon juice (fresh)
- 3 tsp. olive oil
- 1 tbsp. oregano (fresh), cut up
- 1½ tsp. garlic, finely cut up
- 1 tsp. lemon zest, grated
- Salt and powdered black pepper, as desired
- 1 lb. chicken tenders

**For the Sandwiches:**

- 2 (6½-inch) whole-wheat pita breads, halved
- 1 C. spinach (fresh), torn
- 1 C. plum tomatoes, cut up
- ½ of English cucumber, halved and slivered
- ½ C. red onion, slivered

**Procedure of Cooking:**

1. For the marinade: in a large-sized ceramic bowl, put in lemon juice and remnant ingredients except for chicken and blend to incorporate thoroughly.
2. Put in chicken tenders and toss it all to mingle nicely.
3. Cover the bowl and shift into your refrigerator to marinate for around 2 hours.
4. For preheating: set your grill to medium-high heat. Lightly spray the grill grate.
5. Take off the chicken tenders from the bowl and shake off excess marinade.
6. Place the chicken tenders onto the grill. Cook for around 3-4 minutes from both sides.
7. Fill each pita half with chicken, spinach, tomato, cumber and onion.
8. Enjoy immediately.

**Nutritional Facts:**
Calories: 273 | Fat: 7.5g | Carbs: 23.7g | Protein: 28.5g

## Chicken & Veggie Spring Rolls

**Serving Portions:** 4 | **Preparation Period:** 20 mins. | **Cooking Period:** 43 mins.

**Ingredients Required:**

- 3 tbsp. extra-virgin olive oil, divided
- 1 small-sized onion, finely cut up
- 1 clove garlic, finely cut up
- 4 oz. chicken fillet, cut up finely
- 1 C. cabbage, julienned
- 1 C. carrots, peel removed and julienned
- 1 C. string beans, slivered diagonally
- 2 tbsp. water
- Powdered black pepper, as desired
- 8 spring rolls wrappers
- 4 C. lettuce

**Procedure of Cooking:**

1. For preheating: set your oven at 400°F.
2. Lay out bakery paper onto a large-sized baking tray.
3. In a large-sized saucepan, sizzle 2 tbsp. of olive oil on burner at around medium heat.
4. Cook the onion and garlic for around 2 minutes.
5. Put in chicken and cook for around 5 minutes.
6. Put in all the vegetables.
7. Cook for around 15 minutes, mixing time to time.
8. Blend in water and black pepper.
9. Cook for around 1 minute.
10. Take off the pan of chicken mixture from burner and put it aside to cool.
11. Arrange 1 spring roll wrapper onto a smooth surface.
12. Place about 1½-2 tbsp. of chicken mixture over the wrapper in a long rectangle shape.
13. Lightly blend in the wrapper from the sides and then keep rolling until closed tightly.
14. With wet fingertips, dab the wrapper lightly to seal them.
15. Repeat with the remnant wrappers and chicken mixture.
16. Lay out the spring rolls 0nto the baking tray in a single layer.
17. Brush each spring roll with the remnant olive oil.
18. Bake in your oven for around 15-20 minutes.
19. Enjoy warm alongside the lettuce.

**Nutritional Facts:**
Calories: 309 | Fat: 12.8g | Carbs: 36g | Protein: 12.1g

## Chicken & Veggie Kabobs

**Serving Portions:** 4 | **Preparation Period:** 15 mins. | **Cooking Period: 10 mins.**

**Ingredients Required:**

- 1 tsp. powdered cayenne pepper
- 1 tsp. paprika
- ½ tsp. powdered coriander
- 1 tsp. powdered cumin
- Powdered black pepper, as desired
- A tiny 1 pinch of salt
- 2 tsp. balsamic vinegar
- ½ tbsp. olive oil
- 1 lb. boneless chicken breast, cubed
- Olive oil baking spray
- 3 large-sized bell peppers, seeds removed and cut into 1-inch pieces
- 2 C. cherry tomatoes, halved
- 1 medium-sized onion, cut into pieces

**Procedure of Cooking:**

1. For chicken marinade: in a large-sized bowl, blend all together spices, vinegar and oil.
2. Put in chicken cubes and blend with marinade.
3. Cover and shift into your refrigerator for around 1 hour.
4. For preheating: set your oven at 425°F.

5. Spray a large-sized baking tray with baking spray
6. Remove chicken from marinade.
7. Put vegetables in the bowl with marinade and toss to blend.
8. Thread chicken and vegetables onto pre-soaked wooden skewers.
9. Then place the chicken and vegetable skewers onto the baking tray in a single layer.
10. Bake in your oven for around 10 minutes.
11. Enjoy hot.

**Nutritional Facts:**
Calories: 145| Fat: 4.3g| Carbs: 9.1g| Protein: 18.4g

## Herbed Chicken Breast

**Serving Portions:** 6| **Preparation Period:** 15 mins.| **Cooking Period:** 19 mins.

**Ingredients Required:**

- 4 (7-oz.) boneless chicken breasts
- 1 tbsp. olive oil
- 1 tsp. oregano (dried)
- 1 tsp. rosemary (dried)
- 1 tsp. thyme (dried)
- ¼ tsp. garlic powder
- ¼ tsp. onion powder
- 1 tsp. paprika
- Powdered black pepper, as desired

**Procedure of Cooking:**

1. For preheating: set your oven at 425°F.
2. Line a baking pan with bakery paper.
3. With a meat mallet, lb. each chicken breast slightly.
4. In a bowl, blend all together oregano, spices and black pepper.
5. Put in chicken breasts and blend with oil mixture.
6. Lay out the chicken breasts onto the baking pan in a single layer.
7. Bake in your oven for around 16 minutes.

8. Now, set the oven to broiler.
9. Broil the chicken breasts for around 2-3 minutes.
10. Take off the baking pan from oven and place the chicken breasts onto serving plates for 5 minutes before enjoying.
11. Cut each chicken breast into serving slices and enjoy.

**Nutritional Facts:**
Calories: 275| Fat: 12.3g| Carbs: 0.8g| Protein: 38.4g

## Stuffed Chicken Breast

**Serving Portions:** 4| **Preparation Period:** 15 mins.| **Cooking Period:** 25 mins.

**Ingredients Required:**

- 1 tbsp. olive oil
- 1 small-sized onion, cut up
- 1 pepperoni pepper, seeds removed and slivered thinly
- ½ of bell pepper, seeds removed and slivered thinly
- 2 tsp. garlic, finely cut up
- 1 C. spinach leaves (fresh), cut up
- ½ tsp. oregano (dried)
- Salt and powdered black pepper, as desired
- 4 (4-oz.) boneless chicken breasts, butterflied and pounded

**Procedure of Cooking:**

1. For preheating: set your oven at 350°F.
2. Line a baking tray with bakery paper
3. In a saucepan, sizzle the olive oil on burner at around medium heat.
4. Cook the onion and both peppers for around 1 minute.
5. Put in garlic and spinach.
6. Cook for around 2-3 minutes.
7. Blend in oregano, salt and pepper and take off the saucepan from burner.
8. Place the chicken mixture into the middle of each butterflied chicken breast

9. Fold each chicken breast over filling to make a little pocket and secure with toothpicks.
10. Lay out the chicken breasts onto the baking tray.
11. Bake in your oven for around 18-20 minutes
12. Enjoy warm.

**Nutritional Facts:**
Calories: 223 | Fat: 8.7g | Carbs: 3.6g | Protein: 32.3g

## Chicken in Lemon Sauce

**Serving Portions:** 6 | **Preparation Period:** 15 mins. | **Cooking Period:** 1 hr.

**Ingredients Required:**

- 6 chicken thighs
- Salt and powdered black pepper, as desired
- 2 tbsp. extra-virgin olive oil
- ½ of onion, slivered
- 4 C. homemade chicken broth
- 8 sprigs rosemary (fresh)
- ½ tsp. powdered cayenne pepper
- 2 tbsp. arrowroot starch
- 1 tbsp. cold water
- 2 tbsp. lemon juice (fresh)

**Procedure of Cooking:**

1. Rub the chicken with salt and pepper.
2. In a large-sized wok, sizzle the oil on burner at around high heat.
3. Place the chicken thighs, skin side down.
4. Cook for around 3-4 minutes.
5. Shift the thighs onto a plate.
6. In the same wok, put in onion on burner at around medium heat.
7. Cook for around 4-5 minutes.
8. Return the thighs in wok, skin side up.
9. Place broth on top and then then lay out the rosemary sprigs over thighs.
10. Sprinkle with powdered cayenne pepper.

11. Cook the mixture until boiling
12. Immediately turn the heat at around medium-low.
13. Cook with a cover for around 40-45 minutes, coating the thighs with cooking liquid time to time.
14. Meanwhile, in a small-sized bowl, blend all together arrowroot starch and water.
15. Discard the rosemary sprigs and shift the thighs into a bowl.
16. Slowly, put in arrowroot starch mixture, mixing all the time.
17. Blend in the lemon juice.
18. Cook for around 3-4 minutes, mixing time to time.
19. Enjoy hot.

**Nutritional Facts:**
Calories: 296 | Fat: 14.1g | Carbs: 4g | Protein: 36.2g

## Chicken with Mushrooms

**Serving Portions:** 4 | **Preparation Period:** 15 mins. | **Cooking Period:** 20 mins.

**Ingredients Required:**

- 2 tbsp. almond flour
- Salt and powdered black pepper, as desired
- 4 (4-oz.) boneless chicken breasts
- 2 tbsp. olive oil
- 6 cloves garlic, cut up
- ¾ lb. mushrooms (fresh), slivered
- ¾ C. homemade chicken broth
- ¼ C. balsamic vinegar
- 1 bay leaf
- ¼ tsp. thyme (dried)

**Procedure of Cooking:**

1. In a bowl, blend all together flour, salt and pepper.
2. Coat chicken breasts with flour mixture
3. In a wok, sizzle the olive oil on burner at around medium-high heat.

4. Stir-fry the chicken for around 3 minutes.
5. Put in garlic and flip the chicken breasts.
6. Spread mushrooms over chicken.
7. Cook for around 3 minutes, shaking the wok frequently.
8. Put in broth, vinegar, bay leaf and thyme and blend to incorporate.
9. Immediately turn the heat at around medium-low.
10. Cook with a cover for around 10 minutes, flipping chicken time to time.
11. With a frying ladle, shift the chicken onto a warm serving platter.
12. With a piece of heavy-duty foil, cover the chicken to keep warm.
13. Place the pan of sauce on burner at around medium-high heat.
14. Cook for around 7 minutes.
15. Take off the pan from burner and discard the bay leaf.
16. Place mushroom sauce over chicken and enjoy hot.

**Nutritional Facts:**
Calories: 247 | Fat: 11.4g | Carbs: 7.6g | Protein: 29.1g

## Chicken with Broccoli & Spinach

**Serving Portions: 4 | Preparation Period: 15 mins. | Cooking Period: 13 minutes**

**Ingredients Required:**

- 13 oz. coconut milk (unsweetened)
- 1 tsp. ginger root (fresh), grated
- 1½ tsp. curry powder
- 2 tbsp. coconut oil, divide
- 1 lb. boneless chicken breasts, slivered thinly
- 1 large-sized onion, cut up
- 2 C. broccoli florets
- 1 large-sized bunch spinach (fresh), cut up

**Procedure of Cooking:**

1. In a bowl, blend all together coconut milk, ginger and curry powder. Put it aside.
2. In a large-sized wok, sizzle 1 tbsp. of coconut oil on burner at around medium-high heat.
3. Put in chicken and stir-fry for around 3-4 minutes.
4. Shift the chicken into a bowl.
5. In the same wok, sizzle the remnant oil on burner at around medium-high heat.
6. Cook the onion for around 2 minutes.
7. Put in broccoli and stir-fry for around 3 minutes.
8. Put in chicken, spinach and coconut mixture and stir-fry for around 3-4 minutes.
9. Enjoy hot.

**Nutritional Facts:**
Calories: 473 | Fat: 28.6g | Carbs: 13.7g | Protein: 39g

## Chicken & Veggies Stir-fry

**Serving Portions: 6 | Preparation Period: 15 mins. | Cooking Period: 15 mins.**

**Ingredients Required:**

- 3 tbsp. lime juice (fresh)
- 1½ tsp. cornstarch
- 4 tsp. olive oil, divided
- 1 lb. boneless chicken tenders, cubed
- 1 tsp. ginger root (fresh), finely cut up
- 2 cloves garlic, finely cut up
- ¾ tsp. red pepper flakes
- ¼ C. water
- 4 C. broccoli, cut into bite-sized pieces
- 3 C. red bell pepper, seeds removed and slivered
- ¼ C. pine nuts

**Procedure of Cooking:**

1. In a bowl, put in lime juice and cornstarch and blend to incorporate thoroughly. Put it aside.

2. In a large-sized anti-sticking wok, sizzle 2 tsp. of oil on burner at around high heat.
3. Cook chicken about 6-8 minutes, mixing frequently.
4. Shift the chicken into a bowl and put it aside.
5. In the same wok, sizzle remnant oil on burner at around medium heat.
6. Cook ginger, garlic and red pepper flakes for around 1 minute.
7. Put in water, broccoli and bell pepper and stir-fry for around 2-3 minutes.
8. Blend in chicken and lime juice mixture.
9. Cook for around 2-3 minutes.
10. Blend in pine nuts and immediately take off from burner.
11. Enjoy hot.

**Nutritional Facts:**
Calories: 207 | Fat: 10.7g | Carbs: 10.8g | Protein: 20.4g

## Chicken & Tomato Curry

**Serving Portions:** 6 | **Preparation Period:** 15 mins. | **Cooking Period:** 1 hr. 10 mins.

**Ingredients Required:**

- 3 tbsp. olive oil
- 1 medium-sized onion, cut up
- 1 tsp. ginger paste
- 1 tsp. garlic paste
- 4-6 large fresh tomatoes, cut up finely
- 1 tsp. powdered cumin
- 1 pinch of powdered turmeric
- 1½ tsp. red chili powder
- 6 (4-oz.) boneless chicken breast
- 2 C. water, divided
- 2 cardamom pods
- 2 tbsp. cilantro (fresh), cut up

**Procedure of Cooking:**

1. In a large-sized saucepan, sizzle the oil on burner at around medium heat.

2. Cook the onion for around 8-9 minutes.
3. Put in ginger and garlic and sauté for around 1 minute.
4. Put in tomatoes and spices and blend to incorporate.
5. Immediately turn the heat at around medium-low.
6. Cook for around 15-20 minutes, mixing time to time.
7. Take off the pan of tomato mixture from burner and put it aside to cool slightly.
8. In a clean mixer, put in tomato mixture and process to form a smooth mixture.
9. Return the mixture to pan with chicken and ½ C. of the water on burner at around medium-high heat.
10. Cook for around 15-20 minutes, mixing time to time.
11. Put in cardamom pods and remnant water and immediately turn the heat at around low.
12. Cook for around 15-20 minutes.
13. Enjoy hot with the decoration of cilantro.

**Nutritional Facts:**
Calories: 310 | Fat: 15.9g | Carbs: 7.4g | Protein: 34.3g

## Basil Ground Chicken

**Serving Portions:** 4 | **Preparation Period:** 10 mins. | **Cooking Period:** 16 mins.

**Ingredients Required:**

- 2 tbsp. olive oil
- 2 shallots, cut up
- 4 cloves garlic, finely cut up
- ½ tsp. ginger root (fresh), finely cut up
- 1 lb. lean ground chicken
- 2 jalapeño peppers, seeds removed and cut up
- 1 tsp. applesauce
- ½ C. basil (fresh), cut up
- 1 tbsp. lime juice (fresh)
- Salt and powdered black pepper, as desired

**Procedure of Cooking:**

1. In a large-sized wok, sizzle the oil on burner at around medium heat.
2. Cook shallots for around 2-3 minutes.
3. Put in garlic and ginger and sauté for around 1 minutes.
4. Put in chicken and blend.
5. Cook for around 5-7 minutes.
6. Blend in applesauce and basil.
7. Cook for around 3-4 minutes, mixing time to time.
8. Blend in lime juice, salt and pepper and enjoy hot.

**Nutritional Facts:**
Calories: 227 | Fat: 13.2g | Carbs: 3.6g | Protein: 23.7g

## Chicken Meatballs with Broccoli Mash

**Serving Portions:** 5 | **Preparation Period:** 20 mins. | **Cooking Period:** 10 mins.

**Ingredients Required:**

**For the Meatballs:**

- 1 lb. ground chicken
- 2 cloves garlic, finely cut up
- 1 large-sized egg, whisked
- ½ C. low-fat Parmesan cheese, grated freshly
- 2 tbsp. parsley (fresh), cut up
- Salt and powdered black pepper, as desired
- 2 tbsp. olive oil

**For the Broccoli Mash:**

- 1½ C. broccoli florets
- 2 tbsp. basil (fresh), cut up finely
- 1 tbsp. coconut oil, softened
- 1 clove garlic, finely cut up
- Salt and powdered black pepper, as desired

**Procedure of Cooking:**

1. For meatballs: in a large-sized bowl, put in ground chicken and remnant ingredients except for oil and with your hands, mix to incorporate thoroughly.
2. Shape the mixture into balls.
3. In an anti-sticking wok, sizzle the oil on burner at around medium heat.
4. Cook the meatballs for around 10 minutes.
5. With a frying ladle, shift the meatballs onto a plate lined with paper towel.
6. Meanwhile, for broccoli mash: in a saucepan of the lightly salted boiling water, put in broccoli. Cook for around 2-3 minutes.
7. Take off from burner and drain the broccoli thoroughly.
8. In a food mixer, put in broccoli and remnant ingredients and process to form a smooth mixture.
9. Divide the broccoli mash onto serving plates and top with meatballs.
10. Enjoy immediately.

**Nutritional Facts:**
Calories: 253 | Fat: 18.7g | Carbs: 9.8g | Protein: 19.9g

## Chicken Meatballs Curry

**Serving Portions:** 4 | **Preparation Period:** 20 mins. | **Cooking Period:** 30 mins.

**Ingredients Required:**

**For Meatballs:**

- 1 lb. lean ground chicken
- 1 tbsp. onion paste
- 1 tsp. fresh ginger paste
- 1 tsp. garlic paste
- 1green chili, cut up finely
- 1 tbsp. cilantro (fresh) leaves, cut up
- 1 tsp. powdered coriander
- ½ tsp. cumin seeds
- ½ tsp. red chili powder
- ½ tsp. powdered turmeric
- Salt, a needed

**For Curry:**

- tbsp. extra-virgin olive oil
- ½ tsp. cumin seeds
- 1 (1-inch) cinnamon stick
- 3 whole cloves
- 3 whole green cardamoms
- 1 whole black cardamom
- 2 onions, cut up
- 1 tsp. ginger root (fresh), finely cut up
- 1 tsp. garlic, finely cut up
- 4 whole tomatoes, cut up finely
- 2 tsp. powdered coriander
- 1 tsp. garam masala powder
- ½ tsp. powdered nutmeg
- ½ tsp. red chili powder
- ½ tsp. powdered turmeric
- Salt, as desired
- 1 C. water
- 2-3 tbsp. cilantro (fresh), cut up

**Procedure of Cooking:**

1. For meatballs: in a large-sized bowl, put in ground chicken and remnant ingredients and blend to incorporate thoroughly.
2. Make small equal-sized meatballs from mixture.
3. In a large-sized deep wok, sizzle the oil on burner at around medium heat.
4. Cook the meatballs for around 3-5 minutes.
5. Shift the meatballs into a bowl.
6. In the same wok, put in cumin seeds, cinnamon stick, cloves, green cardamom and black cardamom and sauté for around 1 minute.
7. Put in onions and sauté for around 4-5 minutes.
8. Put in ginger and garlic paste and sauté for around 1 minute.
9. Put in tomato and spices.
10. Cook for around 2-3 minutes, crushing with the back of spoon.
11. Put in water and meatballs.
12. Cook the mixture until boiling.
13. Immediately turn the heat at around low.
14. Cook for around 10 minutes.
15. Enjoy hot with the decoration of cilantro.

**Nutritional Facts:**
Calories: 291 | Fat: 17.1g | Carbs: 11.1g | Protein: 24.9g

## Turkey with Cauliflower

**Serving Portions: 4 | Preparation Period: 10 mins. | Cooking Period: 12 mins.**

**Ingredients Required:**

- 1 tbsp. olive oil
- 4 cloves garlic, finely cut up
- 1 lb. boneless turkey breast, cut into small pieces
- 2½ C. cauliflower florets
- 3 tbsp. sugar-free chicken broth
- Powdered black pepper, as desired
- 2 tbsp. cilantro (fresh) leaves, cut up

**Procedure of Cooking:**

1. In a large-sized wok, sizzle the oil on burner at around medium heat.
2. Cook the garlic for around 1 minute.
3. Put in turkey pieces and blend to incorporate.
4. Immediately turn the heat at around medium-high.
5. Cook for around 6-8 minutes.
6. Meanwhile, in a saucepan of boiling water, put in cauliflower.
7. Cook for around 5-6 minutes.
8. Take off from burner and drain the cauliflower thoroughly.
9. Put in cauliflower and broth in wok with beef.
10. Cook for around 2-3 minutes.
11. Blend in the black pepper and take off from burner.
12. Enjoy hot with the decoration of cilantro.

**Nutritional Facts:**
Calories: 162| Fat: 4.8g| Carbs: 4.3g| Protein: 29.8g

---

## Turkey with Bell Pepper & Asparagus

---

**Serving Portions:** 4| **Preparation Period:** 15 mins.| **Cooking Period:** 15 mins.

**Ingredients Required:**

- 4 cloves garlic, finely cut up
- 2 tbsp. lime juice (fresh)
- 1/8 tsp. red pepper flakes
- 1/8 tsp. powdered ginger
- Powdered black pepper, as desired
- 1 bunch asparagus, cut into pieces
- 2 tbsp. olive oil, divided
- 1 lb. boneless turkey breast, slivered thinly
- 1 red bell pepper, seeds removed and slivered
- 3 tbsp. water
- 2 tsp. arrowroot powder

**Procedure of Cooking:**

1. In a bowl, blend all together garlic, lime juice, red pepper flakes, ground ginger and black pepper. Put it aside.
2. In a saucepan of boiling water, cook the asparagus for around 2 minutes.
3. Drain the asparagus and rinse under cold water.
4. In a large-sized wok, sizzle 1 tbsp. of oil on burner at around medium-high heat.
5. Stir-fry the turkey slices for around 3-5 minutes.
6. With a frying ladle, shift the turkey slices into a bowl.
7. In the same wok, sizzle the remnant oil on burner at around medium heat.
8. Stir-fry the asparagus and bell pepper for around 3-4 minutes.
9. Meanwhile, in a bowl, blend all together water and arrowroot powder.
10. In the wok, put in cooked turkey slices, garlic mixture and arrowroot mixture.
11. Cook for around 3-4 minutes, mixing frequently.
12. Enjoy hot.

**Nutritional Facts:**
Calories: 239| Fat: 7.7g| Carbs: 10.2g| Protein: 30.4g

---

## Turkey & Corn Chili

---

**Serving Portions:** 6| **Preparation Period:** 15 mins.| **Cooking Period:** 1 hr.

**Ingredients Required:**

- 2 tbsp. olive oil
- 1 large-sized bell pepper, seeds removed and cut up
- 1 onion, cut up
- 2 cloves garlic, cut up
- 1 lb. lean ground turkey
- 1½ C. water
- 3 C. tomatoes, cut up finely
- 1 tsp. powdered cumin
- ½ tsp. powdered cinnamon
- 2 C. frozen corn, thawed
- ¼ C. scallion greens, cut up

**Procedure of Cooking:**

1. In a large-sized Dutch oven, sizzle the olive oil on burner at around medium-low heat.
2. Cook the bell pepper, onion and garlic for around 5 minutes.
3. Put in turkey and blend.
4. Cook for around 5-6 minutes.
5. Put in water, tomatoes and immediately turn the heat at around high.
6. Cook the mixture until boiling.
7. Immediately turn the heat at around medium-low and blend in corn.
8. Cook with a cover for around 30 minutes, mixing time to time.

9. Enjoy hot with the decoration of scallion greens.

**Nutritional Facts:**
Calories: 226| Fat: 11g| Carbs: 17.3g| Protein: 17.9g

## Turkey Meatballs with Broccoli

**Serving Portions:** 5| **Preparation Period:** 15 mins.| **Cooking Period:** 15 mins.

**Ingredients Required:**

**For Meatballs:**

- 1 lb. 93%-lean ground turkey
- 1 C. frozen cut up spinach, thawed and squeezed
- ½ C. feta cheese, crumbled
- ½ tsp. oregano (dried)
- Salt powdered black pepper, as desired
- 2 tbsp. olive oil

**For Broccoli:**

- 1¼ lb. broccoli florets
- 1 tbsp. olive oil

**Procedure of Cooking:**

1. For meatballs: place ground turkey and remnant ingredients except for oil in a bowl and blend to incorporate thoroughly.
2. Shape the mixture into meatballs.
3. Sizzle the olive oil in a large-sized anti-sticking wok on burner at around medium heat.
4. Cook the meatballs for around 10-15 minutes, flipping time to time.
5. With a frying ladle, shift the meatballs onto a plate.
6. Meanwhile, for broccoli: in a saucepan of boiling water, cook the broccoli for around 3-4 minutes.
7. Drain the broccoli and shift into a bowl.

8. Divide meatballs and broccoli into serving bowls and enjoy.

**Nutritional Facts:**
Calories: 282| Fat: 18.5g| Carbs: 8.5g| Protein: 23.3g

## Turkey & Zucchini Meatloaf

**Serving Portions:** 6| **Preparation Period:** 15 mins.| **Cooking Period:** 50 mins.

**Ingredients Required:**

**For Meatloaf:**

- 1 lb. extra-lean ground turkey
- 1 large-sized egg
- 1 zucchini, shredded finely and squeezed
- 1 medium-sized onion, cut up finely
- 1 bell pepper, seeds removed and cut up finely
- 5 tbsp. gluten-free quick-cooking oats
- 1 tsp. prepared mustard
- 2 tsp. oregano (dried)
- ½ tsp. Italian seasoning
- ½ tsp. garlic powder
- Salt, as desired
- ¼ C. feta cheese, crumbled

**For Sauce:**

- 2 tbsp. homemade tomato paste
- 1 tbsp. water
- 1 tbsp. honey
- Salt, as desired

**Procedure of Cooking:**

1. For preheating: set your oven at 350°F.
2. Lay out bakery paper onto a baking tray
3. For meatloaf: in a large-sized bowl, put in ground turkey and remnant ingredients except for the feta cheese and blend to incorporate thoroughly.

4. Place the turkey mixture 0nto the baking tray and shape into a loaf.
5. With tour fingers, create a long well along the middle of loaf.
6. Place the cheese in the well and cover with the meat mixture firmly.
7. For sauce: in a small-sized bowl, put in tomato paste and remnant ingredients and blend to incorporate thoroughly.
8. Brush 1/3 of the sauce over the meatloaf.
9. Bake in your oven for around 30 minutes.
10. Brush the loaf with another 1/3 of the sauce and bake in your oven for around 20 minutes.
11. Take off from the oven and immediately brush the meatloaf with the remnant sauce.
12. Put it aside for around 5 minutes before enjoying.
13. Divide the meatloaf into desired sized slices and enjoy.

**Nutritional Facts:**
Calories: 163 | Fat: 3.8g | Carbs: 10.1g | Protein: 21

# Meat Recipes

## Beef Pita Pockets

**Serving Portions:** 4 | **Preparation Period:** 15 mins. | **Cooking Period:** 5 mins.

### Ingredients Required:

- 2 cloves garlic, finely cut up
- 1 tbsp. rosemary (fresh), finely cut up
- Salt and powdered black pepper, as desired
- ¾ lb. grass-fed flank steak, fat removed and cut into bite-sized pieces
- 2 tsp. olive oil
- 1 (6-oz.) container fat-free plain Greek yogurt
- 1½ C. cucumber, cut up finely
- 1 tbsp. lemon juice (fresh)
- 4 whole-wheat pita breads, warmed

### Procedure of Cooking:

1. In a bowl, blend all together the garlic, rosemary, salt and pepper.
2. Put in steak cubes and toss it all to mingle nicely.
3. In a large-sized anti-sticking wok, sizzle the oil on burner at around medium-high heat.
4. Cook the lamb for around 4-5 minutes, mixing frequently.
5. Meanwhile, for yogurt sauce: in a bowl, blend all together yogurt, cucumber, lemon juice, salt and pepper.
6. Shift the steak mixture between all the pitas.
7. Enjoy immediately with the drizzling of the yogurt sauce.

### Nutritional Facts:
Calories: 385 | Fat: 10g | Carbs: 38.9g | Protein: 322g

## Beef & Mango Tortillas

**Serving Portions:** 4 | **Preparation Period:** 15 mins.

### Ingredients Required:

- 2 tbsp. lime juice (fresh)
- 2 tbsp. olive oil
- 1 tbsp. Dijon mustard
- Powdered black pepper, as desired
- 2 C. cooked grass-fed beef, shredded
- 1 C. mango, peel removed, pitted and cut into cubes
- 1 C. purple cabbage, shredded
- ¼ C. cilantro (fresh), cut up
- 4 (10-inch) whole-wheat tortillas, warmed

### Procedure of Cooking:

1. In a large-sized bowl, put in mustard, lime juice, oil and black pepper and whisk to incorporate thoroughly.
2. Put in beef, mango, cabbage and cilantro and toss it all to mingle nicely.
3. Lay out the tortillas onto a smooth surface.
4. Place beef mixture over each tortilla, leaving about 1-inch border all around.
5. Carefully, fold the edges of each tortilla over the filling to roll up.
6. Cut each roll in half cross-wise and enjoy.

### Nutritional Facts:
Calories: 296 | Fat: 13.1g | Carbs: 18.3g | Protein: 26.8g

## Simple Steak

**Serving Portions:** 2 | **Preparation Period:** 10 mins. | **Cooking Period:** 10 mins.

**Ingredients Required:**

- 2 (4-oz.) grass-fed sirloin steaks, fat removed
- Salt and powdered black pepper, as desired
- 1 tbsp. extra-virgin olive oil
- 1 clove garlic, finely cut up

**Procedure of Cooking:**

1. Rub the steaks with salt and pepper.
2. In a cast iron wok, sizzle the olive oil on burner at around high heat.
3. Cook the garlic for around 15-20 seconds.
4. Put in steaks and blend.
5. Cook for around 3 minutes from both sides.
6. Flip the steaks.
7. Cook for around 3-4 minutes, flipping once.
8. Enjoy hot.

**Nutritional Facts:**
Calories: 269 | Fat: 16.5g | Carbs: 0.5g | Protein: 30.4g

## Stuffed Steak

**Serving Portions:** 6 | **Preparation Period:** 15 mins. | **Cooking Period:** 38 mins.

**Ingredients Required:**

- Olive oil baking spray
- 1 (1½-lb.) grass-fed flank steak, fat removed
- Powdered black pepper, as desired
- 1 tbsp. olive oil
- 2 small-sized cloves garlic, finely cut up
- 6 oz. spinach (fresh), finely cut up
- 1 medium-sized bell pepper, seeds removed and cut up
- 1 medium-sized tomato, finely cut up

**Procedure of Cooking:**

1. For preheating: set your oven at 425°F.
2. Spray a large-sized baking pan with baking spray.
3. Place the flank steak onto a flat surface.
4. Hold a knife parallel to work surface, slice the steak horizontally, without cutting all the way through, that you can open like a book.
5. With a pounder, flatten the steak to an even thickness.
6. Sprinkle the steak with salt and pepper.
7. In a wok, sizzle the oil on burner at around medium heat.
8. Cook the garlic for around 1 minute.
9. Put in spinach, with salt and pepper.
10. Cook for around 2 minutes.
11. Blend in bell pepper and tomato and immediately take off from burner.
12. Shift the spinach in a bowl and let it cool slightly.
13. Place the filling on the top of steak.
14. Roll up the steak to seal the filling.
15. With cotton twine, tie the steak.
16. Place the steak roll in baking pan.
17. Roast for around 30-35 minutes.
18. Take off from oven and let it cool slightly.
19. Divide the roll in serving portions and enjoy.

**Nutritional Facts:**
Calories: 258 | Fat: 12g | Carbs: 3.7g | Protein: 32.8g

## Steak with Yogurt Sauce

**Serving Portions:** 8 | **Preparation Period:** 15 mins. | **Cooking Period:** 15 mins.

**Ingredients Required:**

- Olive oil baking spray

**For the Steak:**

- 3 cloves garlic, finely cut up
- 2 tbsp. rosemary (fresh), cut up
- Salt and powdered black pepper, as desired
- 2 lb. grass-fed flank steak, fat removed

**For the Sauce:**

- 1½ C. fat-free plain Greek yogurt
- 1 cucumber, peel, seeds removed and finely cut up
- 1 C. parsley (fresh), cut up
- 1 clove garlic, finely cut up
- 1 tsp. fresh lemon zest, finely grated
- 1/8 tsp. powdered cayenne pepper
- Salt and powdered black pepper, as desired

**Procedure of Cooking:**

1. For preheating: set your grill to medium-high heat.
2. Spray the grill grate with baking spray.
3. For steak: in a large-sized bowl, put in the garlic and remnant ingredients except the steak and blend to incorporate thoroughly.
4. Coat the steak with the mixture.
5. Put it aside for around 15 minutes.
6. Place the steak onto the heated grill grate.
7. Cook for around 12-15 minutes, flipping after every 3-4 minutes.
8. Take off the steak from grill and place onto a chopping block for around 5 minutes.
9. Meanwhile, for sauce: in a bowl, put in the yogurt and remnant ingredients and blend to incorporate thoroughly.
10. Divide the steak into serving slices and enjoy alongside yogurt sauce.

**Nutritional Facts:**
Calories: 254 | Fat: 9.7g | Carbs: 6.1g | Protein: 34g

## Steak with Mushrooms

**Serving Portions:** 4 | **Preparation Period:** 15 mins. | **Cooking Period:** 20 mins.

**Ingredients Required:**

**For Steak:**

- 3 tsp. extra-virgin olive oil

- 3 (4-oz.) grass-fed sirloin steaks, fat removed
- 1 pinch of salt
- Powdered black pepper, as desired

**For Mushroom Sauce:**

- 2 tbsp. olive oil
- 2 C. mushrooms (fresh), slivered
- 1 onion, slice
- 2 garlic cloves, peel removed
- 1½ C. salt-free chicken broth

**Procedure of Cooking:**

1. In a large-sized heavy-bottomed wok, sizzle the oil on burner at around high heat.
2. Cook the steaks with salt and black pepper for around 3-5 minutes from both sides.
3. With a frying ladle, Shift the steaks onto a plate
4. With a piece of foil, cover the steaks to keep warm.
5. In the same anti-sticking wok, sizzle the remnant oil on burner at around medium-low heat.
6. Cook the mushrooms, onion and garlic for around 5 minutes, mixing frequently.
7. Blend in the broth.
8. Cook for around 3-5 minutes, mixing frequently.
9. Meanwhile, cut each steak into serving slices.
10. Divide the steak slices onto serving plates and enjoy with the decoration of mushroom sauce.

**Nutritional Facts:**
Calories: 282 | Fat: 21.6g | Carbs: 4.2g | Protein: 29.2g

## Steak with Green Veggies

**Serving Portions:** 5 | **Preparation Period:** 15 mins. | **Cooking Period:** 25 mins.

## Ingredients Required:

- 1 clove garlic, grated
- 1/3 C. plus 3 tbsp. olive oil
- 1/3 C. Dijon mustard
- 1 tbsp. red wine vinegar
- 1 tbsp. water
- 1 tsp. honey
- 1/8 tsp. powdered cayenne pepper
- Salt and powdered black pepper, as desired
- 1 lb. grass-fed boneless strip steak, patted dry
- 1 bunch scallions, slivered thinly and divided
- 4 cloves garlic, slivered
- 1 (10-oz.) bag frozen green peas
- 1 lb. asparagus, cut into 1-inch pieces

## Procedure of Cooking:

1. In a bowl, put in 1 grated clove garlic, ¼ C. of oil, mustard, vinegar, water, honey, powdered cayenne pepper, salt and black pepper and whisk to incorporate thoroughly. Put it aside.
2. Rub the steak with salt and pepper and then, coat with 1 tbsp. of oil
3. Heat a large-sized cast-iron wok on burner at around medium-high heat.
4. Cook the steak for around 10-12 minutes, flipping after every 2 minutes.
5. With a frying ladle, shift the steak onto a plate.
6. Take off the oil from the wok, leaving crispy bits behind.
7. In the same wok, sizzle the remnant oil on burner at around low heat.
8. Cook the scallion and garlic slices for around 3 minutes.
9. Put in green peas and a splash of water.
10. Cook for around 5 minutes, mixing time to time.
11. Put in asparagus, salt and black pepper.
12. Cook for around 5 minutes, mixing time to time.
13. Meanwhile, divide the steak into serving portions.

14. Blend in the steak slices and take off from burner.
15. Shift the steak mixture onto serving plates and drizzle with some mustard sauce.
16. Enjoy alongside the remnant mustard sauce.

## Nutritional Facts:
Calories: 384| Fat: 27.3g| Carbs: 15.5g| Protein: 23.2g

## Steak & Mango Curry

**Serving Portions: 6| Preparation Period: 15 mins.| Cooking Period: 26 mins.**

## Ingredients Required:

- 2 tsp. olive oil
- 16 oz. grass-fed flank steak, fat removed and slivered thinly
- 2 tbsp. salt-free curry paste
- 2 bell peppers, seeds removed and cut into thin strips
- 1 lb. green beans (fresh), fat removed and slivered
- 14 oz. fat-free plain Greek yogurt, whipped
- ¼ C. water
- 1 C. mango, peel removed, pitted and cube
- Powdered black pepper, as desired

## Procedure of Cooking:

1. In an anti-sticking wok, sizzle the oil on burner at around medium-high heat.
2. Cook the beef for around 5-6 minutes.
3. Shift the beef into a bowl.
4. In the same wok, put in curry paste on burner at around medium heat.
5. Cook for around 1 minute.
6. Put in bell peppers and green beans.
7. Cook for around 3-4 minutes.
8. Put in yogurt and water.
9. Cook the mixture until boiling..
10. Cook with a cover for around 5-7 minutes.

11. Blend in mango, cooked beef and black pepper.
12. Cook for around 2-3 minutes.
13. Enjoy hot.

**Nutritional Facts:**
Calories: 287| Fat: 11.2g| Carbs: 16.9g| Protein: 30.3g

## Beef & Lentil Chili

**Serving Portions:** 8| **Preparation Period:** 15 mins.| **Cooking Period:** 1 hr. 5 mins.

**Ingredients Required:**

- 1 tbsp. olive oil
- 2 lb. grass-fed extra-lean ground beef
- 2 C. onion, cut up
- 1 C. bell pepper, seeds removed and cut up
- 1 C. celery stalk, cut up
- 4 cloves garlic, finely cut up
- 1 jalapeño pepper, seeds removed and cut up
- 1 tsp. oregano (dried), crushed
- 2 tbsp. chile powder
- 2 tsp. powdered cumin
- Powdered black pepper, as desired
- 2 bay leaves
- 3 C. tomatoes, finely cut up
- 1 C. homemade chicken broth
- 1 C. water
- 1 C. dried green lentils

**Procedure of Cooking:**

1. In a large-sized pan, sizzle the oil on burner at around medium-high heat.
2. Cook beef for around 3-4 minutes.
3. Put in onion, red pepper, celery, jalapeño, oregano, salt and pepper.
4. Cook for around 5-6 minutes.
5. Put in bay leaves, tomatoes, broth and water.
6. Cook the mixture until boiling.
7. Immediately turn the heat at around medium.

8. Cook with a cover for around 19-20 minutes, mixing time to time.
9. Meanwhile, in another large pan of water, put in lentils.
10. Cook the mixture until boiling.
11. Cook for around 15 minutes, mixing time to time.
12. Drain the lentils and shift into the pan of chili.
13. Cook for around 10 minutes, mixing time to time.
14. Discard bay leaves and enjoy hot.

**Nutritional Facts:**
Calories: 346| Fat: 9.5g| Carbs: 22.3g| Protein: 42.6g

## Ground Beef with Olives

**Serving Portions:** 4| **Preparation Period:** 15 mins.| **Cooking Period:** 15 mins.

**Ingredients Required:**

- 1 tbsp. olive oil
- 1 small-sized onion, cut up finely
- 2 cloves garlic, finely cut up
- Salt and powdered black pepper, as desired
- 1 lb. grass-fed lean ground beef
- 8 oz. spinach (fresh)
- 2 tbsp. oregano (dried)
- 1 tbsp. parsley (dried)
- 8 oz. feta cheese, crumbled
- ¼ C. Kalamata olives, slivered
- ¼ C. green olives, slivered

**Procedure of Cooking:**

1. Preheat the broiler of oven.
2. In a cast iron wok, sizzle the oil on burner at around medium-high heat.
3. Cook the onion, garlic, salt and pepper for around 2-3 minutes.
4. Put in ground beef.
5. Cook for around 4-6 minutes, mixing frequently.
6. Put in spinach and dried herbs and blend to incorporate.

7. Immediately turn the heat at around medium.
8. Cook for around 2-3 minutes.
9. Take off from burner and blend in half of the feta cheese.
10. Place the olives on top of the beef mixture, followed by the remnant feta cheese.
11. Broil for around 2-3 minutes.
12. Take off from the oven and enjoy hot.

**Nutritional Facts:**
Calories: 413| Fat: 21.5g| Carbs: 9.6g| Protein: 44.9g

## Ground Beef with Mushrooms

**Serving Portions:** 4| **Preparation Period:** 15 mins.| **Cooking Period:** 25 mins.

**Ingredients Required:**

- 1 lb. grass-fed lean ground beef
- 2 tbsp. olive oil
- 2 cloves garlic, finely cut up
- ½ of onion, cut up
- 2 C. mushrooms (fresh), slivered
- 2 tbsp. basil (fresh)
- ¼ C. homemade chicken broth
- 2 tbsp. balsamic vinegar
- 2 tbsp. parsley (fresh), cut up

**Procedure of Cooking:**

1. Heat a large-sized anti-sticking wok on burner at around medium-high heat.
2. Cook the ground beef for around 8-10 minutes.
3. With a frying ladle, shift the beef into a bowl.
4. In the same wok, put in onion and garlic for around 3 minutes.
5. Put in mushrooms.
6. Cook for around 5-7 minutes.
7. Put in cooked beef, basil, broth and vinegar.
8. Cook the mixture until boiling.
9. Immediately turn the heat at around medium-low.

10. Cook for around 3 minutes.
11. Blend in parsley and enjoy immediately.

**Nutritional Facts:**
Calories: 289| Fat: 14.2g| Carbs: 3.2g| Protein: 36g

## Ground Beef with Green Peas

**Serving Portions:** 4| **Preparation Period:** 15 mins.| **Cooking Period:** 50 mins.

**Ingredients Required:**

- 1 tbsp. olive oil
- 1 medium-sized onion, cut up
- 1 (¾-inch) piece ginger root (fresh), finely cut up
- 4 cloves garlic, finely cut up
- 1½ tsp. powdered coriander
- ½ tsp. powdered cumin
- ½ tsp. powdered turmeric
- 1 lb. grass-fed lean ground beef
- ½ C. tomato, cut up
- 1½ C. water
- 1 C. fresh green peas, shelled
- 2 tbsp. fat-free Greek yogurt, whipped
- ¼ C. cilantro (fresh), cut up
- Salt and powdered black pepper, as desired

**Procedure of Cooking:**

1. In a Dutch oven, sizzle the oil on burner at around medium-high heat.
2. Cook the onion for around 3-4 minutes.
3. Put in ginger, garlic, ground spices and bay leaf and sauté for around 1 minute.
4. Blend in beef.
5. Cook for around 5 minutes.
6. Blend in tomato.
7. Cook for around 10 minutes, mixing time to time.
8. Blend in water and green peas and bring to a gentle simmer.
9. Immediately turn the heat at around low.

10. Cook with a cover for around 25-30 minutes.
11. Blend in yogurt, cilantro, salt and pepper.
12. Cook for around 4-5 minutes.
13. Enjoy hot.

**Nutritional Facts:**
Calories: 297 | Fat: 12.2g | Carbs: 10.7g | Protein: 35g

## Ground Beef with Barley & Mushrooms

**Serving Portions:** 4 | **Preparation Period:** 15 mins. | **Cooking Period:** 1 hr. 10 mins.

**Ingredients Required:**

- 2 C. water
- ½ C. barley
- 4 tsp. olive oil
- 4 C. fresh button mushrooms, slivered
- Powdered black pepper, as desired
- oz. grass-fed extra-lean ground beef
- 1½ C. onion, cut up
- ½ C. salt-free beef broth
- 4 tbsp. parsley (fresh), cut up

**Procedure of Cooking:**

1. In a Dutch oven, put in water and barley on burner at around medium heat.
2. Cook the mixture until boiling.
3. Immediately turn the heat at around low.
4. Cook with a cover for around 30-40 minutes.
5. Take off the saucepan of barley from burner and put it aside.
6. In a large-sized cast-iron wok, sizzle the oil on burner at around medium-high heat.
7. Cook the beef for around 8-10 minutes.
8. Put in mushroom and onion.
9. Cook for around 5-6 minutes.
10. Put in in mushrooms.
11. Cook for around 2-3 minutes.

12. Blend in cooked barley and broth.
13. Cook for around 3-4 minutes more.
14. Blend in parsley and enjoy hot.

**Nutritional Facts:**
Calories: 342 | Fat: 18.1g | Carbs: 26.4g | Protein: 19.9g

## Beef Meatballs in Tomato Sauce

**Serving Portions:** 8 | **Preparation Period:** 20 mins. | **Cooking Period:** 50 mins.

**Ingredients Required:**

**For the Meatballs:**

- 1¼ lb. grass-fed lean ground beef
- 1 egg
- ¼ C. low-fat Parmesan cheese, grated
- ¼ C. whole-wheat breadcrumbs
- ¼ C. parsley (fresh), cut up finely
- 1 large-sized clove garlic, finely cut up
- Salt, as desired
- 2 tbsp. olive oil

**For the Sauce:**

- 1 tsp. olive oil
- 4 cloves garlic, smashed
- 5 C. tomatoes, finely cut up
- 1 bay leaf
- ½-1 C. water
- Salt and powdered black pepper, as desired
- ¼ C. basil (fresh), cut up

**Procedure of Cooking:**

1. For meatballs: in a large-sized bowl, put in ground beef and remnant ingredients and blend to incorporate thoroughly.
2. Shape the mixture into meatballs.
3. In a large-sized wok, sizzle the oil on burner at around medium heat.
4. Cook the meatballs for around 8-10 minutes, flipping frequently.

5. With a frying ladle, shift the meatballs onto a plate.
6. For sauce: in the same wok, sizzle the olive oil on burner at around medium heat.
7. Cook the garlic for around 1 minute.
8. Put in in the tomatoes.
9. Cook for around 3-4 minutes, crushing with the back of spoon.
10. Put in in bay leaf and water.
11. Cook the mixture until boiling.
12. Blend in the meatballs.
13. Cook the mixture until boiling.
14. Immediately turn the heat at around low.
15. Cook with a cover for around 20-25 minutes.
16. Enjoy hot with the decoration of basil.

**Nutritional Facts:**
Calories: 215| Fat: 9.5g| Carbs: 7.7g| Protein: 24.5g

## Beef Koftas

**Serving Portions:** 6| **Preparation Period:** 20 mins.| **Cooking Period:** 10 mins.

**Ingredients Required:**

**For the Koftas:**

- 1 lb. grass-fed lean ground beef
- 2 tbsp. fat-free plain Greek yogurt
- 2 tbsp. onion, grated
- 2 tsp. garlic, finely cut up
- 2 tbsp. cilantro (fresh), finely cut up
- 1 tsp. powdered coriander
- 1 tsp. powdered cumin
- 1 tsp. powdered turmeric
- Salt and powdered black pepper, as desired
- 1 tbsp. olive oil

**For the Serving:**

- 6 C. lettuce, torn

**Procedure of Cooking:**

1. For koftas: in a large-sized bowl, put in the ground beef and remnant ingredients and blend to incorporate thoroughly.
2. Shape the mixture into 12 oblong shaped patties.
3. In a large-sized anti-sticking wok, sizzle the oil on burner at around medium-high heat.
4. Cook the patties for around 10 minutes, flipping time to time.
5. Divide the lettuce and koftas onto serving plates.
6. Enjoy immediately.

**Nutritional Facts:**
Calories: 176| Fat: 7.3g| Carbs: 3g| Protein: 23.6g

## Beef & Spinach Burgers

**Serving Portions:** 6| **Preparation Period:** 15 mins.| **Cooking Period:** 12 mins.

**Ingredients Required:**

**For the Burgers:**

- 1 lb. grass-fed lean ground beef
- 1 C. fresh baby spinach leaves, cut up
- ½ of small onion, cut up
- ¼ C. sun-dried tomatoes, cut up
- 1 egg, whisked
- ¼ C. feta cheese, crumbled
- Salt and powdered black pepper, as desired
- 2 tbsp. olive oil

**For the Serving:**

- 6 C. fresh salad greens

**Procedure of Cooking:**

1. For burgers: in a large-sized bowl, put in the ground beef and remnant

ingredients except for oil and blend to incorporate thoroughly.
2. Shape the mixture into 4 patties.
3. In a cast-iron wok, sizzle oil on burner at around medium-high heat.
4. Cook the patties for around 5-6 minutes from both sides.
5. Divide the greens onto serving plates and top each with 1 burger.
6. Enjoy immediately.

**Nutritional Facts:**
Calories: 326| Fat: 20.2g| Carbs: 7.9g| Protein: 27.5g

## Beef & Veggie Burgers

**Serving Portions:** 8| **Preparation Period:** 20 mins.| **Cooking Period:** 16 mins.

**Ingredients Required:**

**For the Patties:**

- 1 lb. grass-fed lean ground beef
- 1 carrot, peel removed and cut up finely
- 1 medium-sized raw beetroot, peel removed and cut up finely
- 1 small-sized onion, cut up finely
- 2 Serrano peppers, seeds removed and cut up
- 1 tbsp. cilantro (fresh), cut up finely
- Salt and powdered black pepper, as desired
- 3 tbsp. olive oil

**For the Burgers:**

- 8 whole-wheat hamburger buns, split
- 1 large-sized onion, slivered
- 2 small-sized tomatoes, slivered
- 8 lettuce leaves

**Procedure of Cooking:**

1. For patties: in a large-sized bowl, put in ground beef and remnant ingredients except for oil and blend to incorporate thoroughly.

2. Shape the mixture into 8 patties.
3. In a large-sized anti-sticking wok, sizzle the olive oil on burner at around medium heat.
4. Cook the patties in 2 batches for around 3-4 minutes from both sides.
5. Lay out the bun bottoms onto serving plates.
6. Plce1 patty over each bun, followed by the onion, tomato and lettuce
7. Cover each with top of bun and enjoy.

**Nutritional Facts:**
Calories: 271| Fat: 10.6g| Carbs: 24.2g| Protein: 21.2g

## Ground Beef & Spinach Pinwheel

**Serving Portions:** 6| **Preparation Period:** 20 mins.| **Cooking Period:** 1 hr.

**Ingredients Required:**

**For The Meatloaf:**

- 1¼ lb. grass-fed lean ground beef
- 1 egg, whisked
- ¾ C. whole-wheat breadcrumbs
- Powdered black pepper, as desired

**For the Filling:**

- ¾ C. low-fat Parmesan cheese, shredded
- 1 (10-oz.) bag frozen cut up spinach, thawed and drained
- 1 tsp. Italian seasoning

**For the Topping:**

- 3 tbsp. sugar-free tomato ketchup
- ¼ C. low-fat Parmesan cheese, shredded

**Procedure of Cooking:**

1. For preheating: set your oven at 350°F.
2. Arrange a rack into a roasting pan.
3. Lay out baking paper onto a baking tray.

4. For meatloaf: in a large-sized bowl, put in the ground beef and remnant ingredients and blend to incorporate thoroughly.
5. Place the beef mixture Onto the baking tray and with your hands, shape into a 10x14-inch sized rectangle.
6. With your hands, slightly flatten the mixture.
7. For filling: in another bowl, put in the Parmesan cheese and remnant ingredients and gently blend to incorporate.
8. Place the spinach mixture over turkey rectangle, leaving ¾-inch space from all sides.
9. Pick up the one edge of baking paper and roll it over the meat, starting with the short end.
10. Continue to roll until the meat mixture form in a firm roll, by pulling back the baking paper.
11. Place the roll, seam side down onto the rack in roasting pan.
12. Bake in your oven for around 50 minutes.
13. Take off the roasting pan from oven.
14. Place the ketchup over roll and sprinkle with cheese.
15. Bake in your oven for around 10 minutes more.
16. Take off from the oven and put it aside to cool slightly before slicing.
17. Divide the roll into serving slices and enjoy.

**Nutritional Facts:**
Calories: 264| Fat: 11.7g| Carbs: 14.2g| Protein: 26g

## Beef Stuffed Zucchini

**Serving Portions:** 8| **Preparation Period:** 15 mins.| **Cooking Period:** 50 mins.

**Ingredients Required:**

- 4 medium-sized zucchinis
- 1 lb. grass-fed lean ground beef
- ½ C. onion, cut up
- ½ lb. mushrooms (fresh), slivered
- 1 large-sized tomato, cut up
- 1 egg, whisked
- ¾ C. sugar-free, sugar-free spaghetti sauce
- ¼ C. whole-wheat breadcrumbs
- Powdered black pepper, as desired
- 1 C. part-skim mozzarella cheese, shredded

**Procedure of Cooking:**

1. For preheating: set your oven at 350ºF.
2. Cut each zucchini in half lengthwise.
3. Cut a thin slice from the bottom of each zucchini to allow zucchini to sit flat.
4. With a small-sized spoon, scoop out the pulp from each zucchini half, leaving ¼-inch shells.
5. Shift the zucchini pulp into a large-sized bowl and put it aside.
6. Lay out the zucchini shells into a microwave-safe baking pan.
7. Cover the baking pan and microwave on High for around 3 minutes.
8. Drain the water from microwave and put it aside.
9. Heat a large-sized anti-sticking wok on burner at around medium heat.
10. Cook the ground beef and onion for around 6-7 minutes.
11. Take off the wok of beef from burner and drain the grease.
12. In the bowl of zucchini pulp, put in cooked beef mushrooms, tomato, egg, spaghetti sauce, black pepper and ½ C. of the cheese and blend to incorporate thoroughly.
13. Place about ¼ C. of the beef mixture into each zucchini shell and sprinkle with the remnant cheese.
14. Bake in your oven for around 19-20 minutes.
15. Enjoy warm.

**Nutritional Facts:**
Calories: 219| Fat: 11g| Carbs: 11.6g| Protein: 23.5g

## Beef Stuffed Bell Peppers

**Serving Portions: 6 | Preparation Period: 15 mins. | Cooking Period: 40 mins.**

**Ingredients Required:**

- 3 large-sized bell peppers, halved lengthwise and seeds removed
- 1 C. chicken broth
- ½ C. dry quinoa, rinsed
- 4 tbsp. olive oil, divided
- ½ lb. grass-fed lean ground beef
- ½ C. red onion, cut up
- 2 tbsp. garlic, crushed
- Salt and powdered black pepper, as desired
- ¼ C. pine nuts, toasted
- ¼ C. Kalamata olives, roughly cut up
- ¼ C. sun-dried tomatoes, cut up
- 2 tbsp. capers, drained
- 1 tbsp. lemon juice (fresh)
- 1 tsp. parsley (dried)
- ½ tsp. basil (dried)
- ½ tsp. oregano (dried)
- ¼ C. feta cheese, crumbled

**Procedure of Cooking:**

1. For preheating: set your oven at 375°F.
2. Lay out a piece of heavy-duty aluminium foil onto a baking tray.
3. In a saucepan, put in broth and quinoa on burner at around medium heat.
4. Cook the mixture until boiling.
5. Immediately turn the heat at around low.
6. Cook with a cover for around 15 minutes, mixing time to time.
7. Take off from burner and with a fork, fluff the quinoa.
8. Meanwhile, in a large-sized pan, sizzle 2 tbsp. of oil on burner at around medium heat.
9. Cook the beef for around 4-5 minutes.
10. Put in onion and garlic.
11. Cook for around 5-7 minutes.
12. Blend in the salt and pepper and take off from burner.
13. Take off from burner and put it aside to cool slightly.
14. In a large-sized bowl, put in cooked quinoa, beef mixture, pine nuts, olives, sun-dried tomatoes, capers, lemon juice, dried herbs, salt and pepper and blend to incorporate thoroughly.
15. Rub the insides and outsides of each bell pepper with remnant olive oil.
16. Lay out the bell pepper halves onto the baking tray, cut side facing up.
17. Sprinkle each half with salt and pepper.
18. Place turkey mixture in each bell pepper half.
19. Bake in your oven for around 20-25 minutes.
20. Take off from the oven and immediately sprinkle with feta cheese.
21. Enjoy immediately.

**Nutritional Facts:**
Calories: 304 | Fat: 20.6g | Carbs: 17.5g | Protein: 15g

# Fish & Seafood Recipes

## Tuna Stuffed Avocado

**Serving Portions:** 2 | **Preparation Period:** 10 mins.

**Ingredients Required:**

- 1 large-sized avocado, halved
- 1 tbsp. onion, finely cut up
- 2 tbsp. fresh lemon juice
- 4 oz. cooked tuna
- Powdered black pepper, as desired

**Procedure of Cooking:**

1. Scoop out the flesh from the middle of avocado and shift into a bowl.
2. Put in onion and lemon juice and mash until thoroughly blended.
3. Put in tuna and black pepper and blend to incorporate.
4. Divide the tuna mixture into each avocado half and enjoy immediately.

**Nutritional Facts:**
Calories: 256 | Fat: 8.56g | Carbs: 6.9g | Protein: 16.6g

## Tuna Lettuce Wraps

**Serving Portions:** 4 | **Preparation Period:** 15 mins.

**Ingredients Required:**

- 1 (6-oz.) can water-packed white tuna, drained
- 2 tbsp. low-fat mayonnaise
- 1 pinch of salt
- Powdered black pepper, as desired
- 1 medium-sized bell pepper, seeds removed and cut up
- ¼ C. scallion, cut up
- 1 tbsp. cilantro (fresh), cut up
- ¼ tsp. lemon juice (fresh)
- 8 large romaine lettuce leaves
- ½ C. tomato, cut up

**Procedure of Cooking:**

1. In a large-sized bowl, blend all together tuna, mayonnaise, salt and pepper.
2. Put in bell pepper, scallion, cilantro and lemon juice and blend to incorporate.
3. Place the lettuce leaves onto serving plates.
4. Divide the tuna mixture over each leaf.
5. Top with tomato and enjoy immediately.

**Nutritional Facts:**
Calories: 100 | Fat: 3.9g | Carbs: 5.7g | Protein: 10.8g

## Simple Salmon

**Serving Portions:** 2 | **Preparation Period:** 10 mins. | **Cooking Period: 8 mins.**

**Ingredients Required:**

- 2 (5-oz.) (1-inch thick) salmon fillets
- Salt and powdered black pepper, as desired
- 1 tbsp. extra-virgin olive oil
- 2 tbsp. cilantro (fresh) leaves, cut up

**Procedure of Cooking:**

1. Rub the salmon fillets with salt and pepper.
2. In a large-sized wok, sizzle the oil on burner at around medium-high heat.
3. Place the salmon, skins side up.
4. Cook for around 4 minutes.

5. Carefully change the side of fillets.
6. Cook for around 4 minutes more.

**Nutritional Facts:**
Calories: 248| Fat: 15.8g| Carbs: 0.1g| Protein: 27.5g

## Garlicky Salmon

**Serving Portions:** 5| **Preparation Period:** 10 mins.| **Cooking Period:** 8 mins.

**Ingredients Required:**

- 2 tbsp. olive oil
- 5 (5-oz.) salmon fillets
- 3 cloves garlic, finely cut up
- 1 tbsp. ginger root (fresh), finely cut up
- 2-3 tbsp. salt-free chicken broth
- Salt and powdered black pepper, as desired

**Procedure of Cooking:**

1. In a large-sized wok, sizzle the oil on burner at around medium heat.
2. Cook the salmon fillets for around 3 minutes.
3. Change the side and blend in the garlic and ginger.
4. Cook for around 1-2 minutes.
5. Put in broth and bend.
6. Cook for around 2-3 more minutes.
7. Take off from burner and enjoy hot.

**Nutritional Facts:**
Calories: 162| Fat: 5.9g| Carbs: 0.8g| Protein: 26.7g

## Spiced Salmon

**Serving Portions:** 6| **Preparation Period:** 10 mins.| **Cooking Period:** 8 mins.

**Ingredients Required:**

- ½ tbsp. powdered ginger
- ½ tbsp. powdered coriander

- ½ tbsp. powdered cumin
- ½ tsp. paprika
- ¼ tsp. powdered cayenne pepper
- Salt, as desired
- 1 tbsp. orange juice (fresh)
- 1 tbsp. coconut oil, liquefied
- 1½-2 lb. salmon fillets
- Olive oil baking spray

**Procedure of Cooking:**

1. In a large-sized bowl, put in powdered ginger and remnant ingredients except for salmon and blend to form a paste.
2. Put in salmon and blend with mixture.
3. Shift into your refrigerator to marinate for around 30 minutes.
4. For preheating: set your gas grill to high heat with the lid closed for at least 10 minutes.
5. Spray the grill grate with baking spray.
6. Place the salmon fillets, skin-side down onto the grill.
7. Cover the grill with the lid.
8. Cook for around 3-4 minutes from both sides.
9. Enjoy hot.

**Nutritional Facts:**
Calories: 175| Fat: 9.5g| Carbs: 1g| Protein: 22.2g

## Sweet & Sour Salmon

**Serving Portions:** 4| **Preparation Period:** 10 mins.| **Cooking Period:** 12 mins.

**Ingredients Required:**

- 2 cloves garlic, crushed
- 2 tbsp. ginger root (fresh), finely grated
- 2 tbsp. honey
- 2 tbsp. lime juice (fresh)
- 3 tbsp. olive oil
- 2 tbsp. black sesame seeds
- 1 tbsp. white sesame seeds
- 1 lb. boneless salmon fillets
- 1/3 C. scallion, cut up

**Procedure of Cooking:**

1. In a baking pan, put in garlic and remnant ingredients except for the salmon and scallion.
2. Put in salmon and blend with mixture.
3. Shift into your refrigerator to marinate for around 40-45 minutes.
4. Preheat the broiler of oven.
5. Place the baking pan in the oven and broil for around 10-12 minutes.
6. Take off the baking pan from oven and Shift the salmon fillets onto a serving platter.
7. Top the salmon fillets with the pan sauce and Decorate with scallion.
8. Enjoy immediately.

**Nutritional Facts:**
Calories: 324 | Fat: 20.9g | Carbs: 12.9g | Protein: 23.5g

## Cheesy Salmon Parcel

**Serving Portions:** 4 | **Preparation Period:** 10 mins. | **Cooking Period:** 25 mins.

**Ingredients Required:**

- 2 cloves garlic, crushed
- 1 tsp. dried dill weed, crushed
- Salt and powdered black pepper, as desired
- 4 (5-oz.) salmon fillets
- ½ C. low-fat cheddar cheese, shredded
- 4 scallions, cut up

**Procedure of Cooking:**

1. For preheating: set your oven at 450°F.
2. In a bowl, blend all together garlic, dill weed, salt and pepper.
3. Rub the salmon fillets with garlic mixture.
4. Lay out the salmon fillets over a large-sized piece of foil and then fold it to seal.
5. Place the salmon parcel onto a baking tray.

6. Bake in your oven for around 20 minutes.
7. Now, unfold the parcel and top the salmon fillets with cheese and scallions.
8. Bake in your oven for around 5 minutes.
9. Enjoy hot.

**Nutritional Facts:**
Calories: 252 | Fat: 13.5g | Carbs: 1.9g | Protein: 31.4g

## Salmon in Spicy Yogurt Sauce

**Serving Portions:** 5 | **Preparation Period:** 15 mins. | **Cooking Period:** 35 mins.

**Ingredients Required:**

- 5 (4-oz.) salmon fillets
- 1½ tsp. powdered turmeric, divided
- Salt, as desired
- 3 tbsp. coconut oil, divided
- 1 (1-inch) stick cinnamon, pounded roughly
- 3-4 green cardamom, pounded roughly
- 4-5 whole cloves, pounded roughly
- 2 bay leaves
- 1 onion, cut up finely
- 1 tsp. garlic paste
- 1½ tsp. fresh ginger paste
- 3-4 green chilies, halved
- 1 tsp. red chili powder
- ¾ C. fat-free plain Greek yogurt
- ¾ C. water
- ¼ C. cilantro (fresh), cut up

**Procedure of Cooking:**

1. In a bowl, season the salmon with ½ tsp. of the turmeric and salt and put it aside.
2. In a large-sized, anti-sticking wok, sizzle 1 tbsp. of coconut oil on burner at around medium heat.
3. Cook salmon fillets for around 2-3 minutes from both sides.
4. Shift the salmon fillets into a bowl.

5. In the same wok, sizzle remnant oil on burner at around medium heat.
6. Cook cinnamon, green cardamom, whole cloves and bay leaves for around 1 minute.
7. Put in onion and sauté for around 4-5 minutes.
8. Put in garlic paste, ginger paste, green chilies and sauté for around 2 minutes.
9. Immediately turn the heat at around medium-low.
10. Put in remnant turmeric, red chili powder and salt and sauté for around 1 minute.
11. Meanwhile, in a bowl, put in yogurt and water and whisk to form a smooth mixture.
12. Immediately turn the heat at around low and slowly, put in yogurt mixture, mixing all the time.
13. Cook with a cover for around 15 minutes.
14. Put in in the salmon fillets.
15. Cook for around 5 minutes.
16. Enjoy hot with the decoration of cilantro.

**Nutritional Facts:**
Calories: 313 | Fat: 18.3g | Carbs: 1.4g | Protein: 34g

## Salmon with Peach

**Serving Portions:** 4 | **Preparation Period:** 15 mins. | **Cooking Period:** 12 mins.

**Ingredients Required:**

- Olive oil baking spray
- 4 (5-oz.) salmon fillets
- Salt and powdered black pepper, as desired
- 3 peaches, pitted and cut into wedges
- 2 medium-sized red onions, cut into wedges
- 1 tbsp. ginger root (fresh), finely cut up
- 1 tsp. thyme (fresh) leaves, finely cut up
- 3 tbsp. olive oil
- 1 tbsp. balsamic vinegar

**Procedure of Cooking:**

1. For preheating: set your grill to medium heat.
2. Spray the grill grate with baking spray.
3. Rub the salmon fillets with salt and pepper.
4. In a bowl, put in peaches, onion, salt and pepper and toss it all to mingle nicely.
5. Place the salmon fillets onto the grill.
6. Cook for around 5-6 minutes from both sides.
7. Place peaches and onions onto the grill with salmon fillets.
8. Cook for around 3-4 minutes from both sides.
9. Meanwhile, in a bowl, put in remnant ingredients and mix until a smooth paste forms.
10. Place ginger mixture over salmon filets and enjoy with peaches and onions.

**Nutritional Facts:**
Calories: 350 | Fat: 19.7g | Carbs: 16.8g | Protein: 29.3g

## Spicy Cod

**Serving Portions:** 4 | **Preparation Period:** 10 mins. | **Cooking Period:** 14 mins.

**Ingredients Required:**

- Olive oil baking spray
- ¼ C. fat-free plain Greek yogurt
- tsp. powdered coriander
- ½ tsp. powdered turmeric
- ½ tsp. powdered ginger
- ¼ tsp. powdered cayenne pepper
- Salt and powdered black pepper, as desired
- 4 (6-oz.) skinless cod fillets

**Procedure of Cooking:**

1. For preheating: set your oven to broiler.
2. Spray a broiler pan with baking spray.

3. In a large-sized bowl, blend all together yogurt, spices, salt and pepper.
4. Lay out salmon fillets 0nto the broiler pan.
5. Place the yogurt mixture over each fillet.
6. Broil for around 12-14 minutes.
7. Enjoy immediately.

**Nutritional Facts:**
Calories: 146 | Fat: 1.6g | Carbs: 1.5g | Protein: 31g

## Tilapia with Veggies

**Serving Portions:** 2 | **Preparation Period:** 15 mins. | **Cooking Period:** 15 mins.

**Ingredients Required:**

- 1 (8-oz.) tilapia fillet, cubed
- ¼ tsp. ginger paste
- ¼ tsp. garlic paste
- 1 tsp. red chili powder
- Salt, as desired
- 1 tbsp. coconut vinegar
- 1 tbsp. extra-virgin olive oil, divided
- ½ C. mushrooms (fresh), slivered
- 1 small-sized onion, quartered
- ½ C. bell pepper, seeds removed and cubed
- 2-3 scallions, cut up

**Procedure of Cooking:**

1. In a bowl, blend all together tilapia, ginger, garlic, chili powder and salt and put it aside for around 20 minutes.
2. In an anti-sticking wok, sizzle 1 tsp. of oil on burner at around medium-high heat.
3. Sear the tilapia cubes for around 3-4 minutes.
4. In another wok, sizzle remnant oil on burner at around medium heat.
5. Stir-fry the mushrooms and onion for around 5-7 minutes.

6. Put in bell pepper and tilapia cubes.
7. Stir-fry for around 2 minutes.
8. Put in scallion and stir-fry for bout 1-2 minutes.
9. Enjoy hot.

**Nutritional Facts:**
Calories: 193 | Fat: 8.5g | Carbs: 8.2g | Protein: 23.5g

## Shrimp Lettuce Wraps

**Serving Portions:** 4 | **Preparation Period:** 15 mins. | **Cooking Period:** 5 mins.

**Ingredients Required:**

- 1 tsp. extra-virgin olive oil
- 1 clove garlic, finely cut up
- 1½ lb. shrimp, peeled, deveined and cut up
- Salt, as desired
- 8 large lettuce leaves
- 1 tbsp. chives (fresh), finely cut up

**Procedure of Cooking:**

1. In a large-sized wok, sizzle the olive oil on burner at around medium heat.
2. Cook garlic for around 1 minute.
3. Put in shrimp and blend.
4. Cook for around 3-4 minutes.
5. Take off from burner and put it aside to cool slightly.
6. Arrange lettuce leaves onto serving plates.
7. Divide the shrimp over the leaves.
8. Decorate with chives and enjoy immediately.

**Nutritional Facts:**
Calories: 215 | Fat: 4.4g | Carbs: 3.2g | Protein: 38.9g

## Shrimp with Zucchini & Tomato

**Serving Portions:** 4 | **Preparation Period:** 15 mins. | **Cooking Period:** 8 mins.

**Ingredients Required:**

- 2 tbsp. olive oil
- 1 clove garlic, finely cut up
- ¼ tsp. red pepper flakes
- 1 lb. shrimp, peeled and deveined
- Powdered black pepper, as desired
- 1/3 C. homemade chicken broth
- 2 medium-sized zucchinis, spiralized with blade C
- 1 C. cherry tomatoes, quartered

**Procedure of Cooking:**

1. In a large-sized anti-sticking wok, sizzle the olive oil on burner at around medium heat.
2. Cook garlic and red pepper flakes for around 1 minute.
3. Put in shrimp and black pepper.
4. Cook for around 1 minute from both sides.
5. Put in broth and zucchini noodles.
6. Cook for around 3-4 minutes.
7. Blend in tomato quarters and take off from burner.
8. Enjoy hot.

**Nutritional Facts:**
Calories: 221| Fat: 9.2g| Carbs: 7.2g| Protein: 27.7g

## Shrimp with Broccoli

**Serving Portions:** 6| **Preparation Period:** 15 mins.| **Cooking Period:** 12 mins.

**Ingredients Required:**

- 2 tbsp. coconut oil, divided
- 4 C. broccoli, cut up
- 2 lb. large shrimp, peeled and deveined
- 2 cloves garlic, finely cut up
- 1 (1-inch) piece ginger root (fresh), finely cut up
- Salt and powdered black pepper, as desired

**Procedure of Cooking:**

1. In a large-sized wok, sizzle 1 tbsp. of coconut oil on burner at around medium-high heat.
2. Cook the broccoli for around 3-4 minutes.
3. With the spoon, push the broccoli to the sides of pan.
4. In the center of wok, put in remnant coconut oil and let it sizzle and blend
5. Put in shrimp.
6. Cook for around 2-3 minutes, tossing time to time.
7. Put in in garlic, ginger, salt and pepper.
8. Cook for around 2-3 minutes, mixing time to time.
9. Enjoy hot.

**Nutritional Facts:**
Calories: 241| Fat: 7.3g| Carbs: 6.7g| Protein: 36.2g

## Shrimp with Bell Peppers & Mushrooms

**Serving Portions:** 4| **Preparation Period:** 20 mins.| **Cooking Period:** 12 mins.

**Ingredients Required:**

- 2 tbsp. olive oil
- 4 cloves garlic, finely cut up
- 1 fresh red chili, slivered
- 1 lb. medium shrimp, peeled and deveined
- ½ C. mushrooms (fresh), slivered
- 2 C. bell peppers, seeds removed and julienned
- ½ C. onion, slivered thinly
- ¼ C. homemade chicken broth
- ¼ C. scallion, cut up
- Powdered black pepper, as desired

**Procedure of Cooking:**

1. In a large-sized anti-sticking wok, sizzle olive oil on burner at around medium heat.
2. Cook the garlic and red chili for around 2 minutes.
3. Put in mushrooms.
4. Cook for around 4-5 minutes.
5. Put in shrimp, bell peppers, onion and black pepper and stir-fry for around 5 minutes.
6. Blend in broth.
7. Cook for around 1 minute.
8. Blend in scallion and take off from burner.
9. Enjoy hot.

**Nutritional Facts:**
Calories: 202| Fat: 8.6g| Carbs: 7.7g| Protein: 25.8g

## Shrimp & Veggies Stir-fry

**Serving Portions:** 4| **Preparation Period:** 20 mins.| **Cooking Period:** 10 mins.

**Ingredients Required:**

- 2 tbsp. olive oil, divided
- 1 lb. large shrimp, peeled and deveined
- ½ of onion, cut up
- 3 cloves garlic, finely cut up
- 2 C. broccoli floret
- 1 C. fresh snow peas
- 1 C. carrot, peel removed and julienned
- 2 tbsp. water
- Salt and powdered black pepper, as desired
- 2 tbsp. parsley (fresh), cut up

**Procedure of Cooking:**

1. In a large-sized anti-sticking wok, sizzle 1 tbsp. of olive oil on burner at around medium heat.
2. Cook the shrimp for around 1 minute from both sides.
3. With a frying ladle, shift the shrimp onto a plate.

4. In the same wok, sizzle the remnant oil on burner at around medium heat.
5. Cook the onion and garlic for around 2-3 minutes.
6. Put in vegetables, water, salt and pepper and stir-fry for around 2-3 minutes.
7. Blend in the cooked shrimp and stir-fry for around 1-2 minutes.
8. Enjoy hot.

**Nutritional Facts:**
Calories: 250| Fat: 9.2g| Carbs: 12.9g| Protein: 29.5g

## Shrimp & Tomato Curry

**Serving Portions:** 4| **Preparation Period:** 15 mins.| **Cooking Period:** 16 mins.

**Ingredients Required:**

- 2 tbsp. olive oil
- ½ sweet onion, finely cut up
- 2 cloves garlic, finely cut up
- 1½ tsp. powdered turmeric
- 1 tsp. powdered cumin
- 1 tsp. powdered ginger
- 1 tsp. paprika
- ½ tsp. red chili powder
- 1 (14-oz.) can coconut milk (unsweetened)
- 2½ cups tomatoes, finely cut up
- Salt, as desired
- 1 lb. cooked shrimp
- 2 tbsp. cilantro (fresh), cut up

**Procedure of Cooking:**

1. In a large-sized wok, sizzle the oil on burner at around medium-low heat.
2. Cook the onion for around 5 minutes.
3. Put in garlic and spices and sauté for around 1 minute.
4. Put in coconut milk, tomatoes and salt.
5. Cook for around 4-5 minutes, mixing time to time.
6. Blend in the shrimp and cilantro.

7. Cook for around 4-5 minutes.
8. Enjoy hot.

**Nutritional Facts:**
Calories: 243 | Fat: 10.5g | Carbs: 9.7g | Protein: 27.5g

## Shrimp, Fruit & Bell Pepper Curry

**Serving Portions:** 6 | **Preparation Period:** 15 mins. | **Cooking Period:** 15 mins.

**Ingredients Required:**

- 2 tbsp. coconut oil
- ½ C. onion, slivered thinly
- 1½ lb. shrimp, peeled and deveined
- ½ of bell pepper, seeds removed and slivered thinly
- 1 mango, peel removed, pitted and slivered
- 8 oz. can of pineapple tidbits with unsweetened juice
- 1 C. coconut milk (unsweetened)
- 1 tbsp. red curry paste
- 2 tbsp. cilantro (fresh), cut up

**Procedure of Cooking:**

1. In a large-sized, anti-sticking saucepan, sizzle coconut oil on burner at around medium-high heat.
2. Cook the onion for around 3-4 minutes.
3. Put in in shrimp and blend. Cook for around 2 minutes from both sides.
4. Put in bell peppers.
5. Cook for around 3-4 minutes.
6. Put in remnant ingredients except for cilantro.
7. Cook for around 5 minutes.
8. Enjoy hot with the decoration of cilantro.

**Nutritional Facts:**
Calories: 311 | Fat: 14g | Carbs: 19.7g | Protein: 27.9g

## Rosemary Scallops

**Serving Portions:** 3 | **Preparation Period:** 15 mins. | **Cooking Period:** 5 mins.

**Ingredients Required:**

- 2 tbsp. olive oil
- 2 tbsp. rosemary (fresh), cut up
- 2 cloves garlic, finely cut up
- 1 lb. sea scallops
- 1 pinch of salt
- Powdered black pepper, as desired

**Procedure of Cooking:**

1. In a medium-sized wok, sizzle the oil on burner at around medium-high heat.
2. Cook the rosemary and garlic for around 1 minute.
3. Put in scallops and blend.
4. Cook for around 2 minutes from both sides.
5. Enjoy hot.

**Nutritional Facts:**
Calories: 223 | Fat: 10.8g | Carbs: 5.7g | Protein: 25.6g

## Scallops with Veggies

**Serving Portions:** 2 | **Preparation Period:** 15 mins. | **Cooking Period:** 15 mins.

**Ingredients Required:**

- ¾ C. homemade chicken broth, divided
- 1 C. carrot, peel removed and cut up
- 1 C. celery cut up
- 1½ C. green beans, cut up
- ¾ of green apple, cored and cut up
- ½ tsp. ginger root (fresh), finely grated
- 1 tsp. powdered cardamom
- Salt and powdered black pepper, as desired
- 2 tsp. olive oil
- 8 oz. sea scallops, side muscles removed

**Procedure of Cooking:**

1. In a large-sized wok, put in ¼ C. of broth.
2. Cook the mixture until boiling.
3. Put in in the carrots and celery.
4. Cook for around 4-5 minutes.
5. Blend in green beans, apple, ginger, cardamom, salt, black pepper and remnant broth.
6. Cook for around 3-4 minutes.
7. Meanwhile in a frying pan, sizzle the oil.
8. Cook the scallops for around 2-3 minutes from both sides.
9. Shift the scallops into the wok with veggie mixture and blend to incorporate.
10. Enjoy immediately.

**Nutritional Facts:**
Calories: 326| Fat: 6.7g| Carbs: 43.8g| Protein: 27.5g

# Vegetarian Recipes

## Zucchini Lettuce Wraps

**Serving Portions:** 4 | **Preparation Period:** 15 mins. | **Cooking Period:** 14 mins.

**Ingredients Required:**

- 1 tbsp. olive oil
- 1 tsp. cumin seeds
- 1 small-sized onion, slivered thinly
- 4 C. zucchini, grated
- ½ tsp. red pepper flakes
- Salt and powdered black pepper, as desired
- 8 large lettuce leaves, rinsed and pat dried
- 2 tbsp. chives (fresh), finely cut up finely

**Procedure of Cooking:**

1. In a medium-sized wok, sizzle the oil on burner at around medium-high heat.
2. Cook the cumin seeds for around 1 minute.
3. Put in onion and sauté for around 4-5 minutes.
4. Put in zucchini.
5. Cook for around 5-7 minutes, mixing time to time.
6. Blend in the red pepper flakes, salt and pepper and take off from burner.
7. Lay out the lettuce leaves onto a smooth surface.
8. Divide the zucchini mixture onto each lettuce leaf.
9. Top with the chives and enjoy immediately.

**Nutritional Facts:**
Calories: 60 | Fat: 3.9g | Carbs: 6.2g | Protein: 1.8g

## Quinoa Lettuce Wraps

**Serving Portions:** 4 | **Preparation Period:** 15 mins. | **Cooking Period:** 10 mins.

**Ingredients Required:**

**For the Filling:**

- 1 tsp. olive oil
- 2 C. fresh shiitake mushrooms, cut up
- 1 C. cooked quinoa
- 1 tsp. fresh lime juice
- 1 tsp. balsamic vinegar
- ¼ C. scallion, cut up
- 1 pinch of salt
- Powdered black pepper, as desired

**For the Wraps:**

- 8 butter lettuce leaves
- ¼ C. cucumber, peel removed and julienned
- ¼ C. carrot, peel removed and julienned
- 2 tbsp. unsalted peanuts, cut up

**Procedure of Cooking:**

1. For filling in a wok, sizzle the oil on burner at around medium heat.
2. Cook the mushrooms for around 5-8 minutes.
3. Blend in quinoa, lime juice and vinegar.
4. Cook for around 1 minute.
5. Blend in scallion, salt and black pepper and immediately take off from burner.
6. Let it cool.
7. Place lettuce leaves into serving plates.
8. Place quinoa filling over each leaf.
9. Top with cucumber, carrot and peanuts and enjoy.

**Nutritional Facts:**
Calories: 176| Fat: 5.4g| Carbs: 25.8g| Protein: 7.2g

## Veggie Tortilla Wraps

**Serving Portions:** 4| **Preparation Period:** 15 mins.| **Cooking Period:** 22 mins.

**Ingredients Required:**

- 1½ C. broccoli florets, cut up
- 1½ C. cauliflower florets, cut up
- 1 tbsp. water
- 2 tsp. olive oil
- 1½ C. onion, cut up
- 1 clove garlic, finely cut up
- 2 tbsp. parsley (fresh), finely cut up
- 4 egg, whisked
- Salt and powdered black pepper, as desired
- 4 whole-wheat tortillas, warmed

**Procedure of Cooking:**

1. In a microwave-safe bowl, put in broccoli, cauliflower and water.
2. Microwave with a cover for around 3-5 minutes.
3. Take off from microwave and drain any liquid.
4. Sizzle olive oil in a wok on burner at around medium heat.
5. Cook the onion for around 4-5 minutes.
6. Put in garlic and sauté for around 1 minute.
7. Blend in broccoli, cauliflower, parsley, eggs, salt and pepper.
8. Immediately turn the heat at around medium-low.
9. Cook for around 10 minutes.
10. Take off the wok of veggies from burner and put it aside to cool slightly.
11. Place broccoli mixture over ¼ of each tortilla.
12. Fold the outside edges inward and roll up like a burrito.

13. Secure the tortilla with toothpicks to secure the filling.
14. Cut each tortilla in half and enjoy.

**Nutritional Facts:**
Calories: 147| Fat: 3.2g| Carbs: 19.8g| Protein: 11.2g

## Stuffed Zucchini

**Serving Portions:** 8| **Preparation Period:** 15 mins.| **Cooking Period:** 23 mins.

**Ingredients Required:**

- 4 medium-sized zucchinis, halved lengthwise
- Salt, as desired
- 1½ baking potatoes, peel removed and cubed
- 4 tsp. olive oil
- 2½ C. onion, cut up
- 1 Serrano chile, mined
- 2 cloves garlic, finely cut up
- 1½ tbsp. ginger root (fresh), finely cut up
- 2 tbsp. almond flour
- 1 tsp. powdered coriander
- ¼ tsp. powdered cumin
- ¼ tsp. powdered turmeric
- Powdered black pepper, as desired
- 1½ C. frozen green peas, thawed
- 2 tbsp. cilantro (fresh), cut up

**Procedure of Cooking:**

1. For preheating: set your oven at 375°F.
2. With a scooper, scoop out the pulp from zucchini halves, leaving about ¼-inch thick shell.
3. In a shallow roasting pan, lay out the zucchini halves, cut side up.
4. Sprinkle the zucchini halves with a little salt.
5. In a saucepan of boiling water, cook the potatoes for around 2 minutes.

6. Drain the potatoes well and put it aside.
7. In a large-sized anti-sticking wok, sizzle the oil on burner at around medium-high heat.
8. Cook the onion, Serrano, garlic and ginger for around 3 minutes.
9. Immediately turn the heat at around medium-low and blend in almond flour and spices.
10. Cook for around 5 minutes, mixing all the time.
11. Sir in cooked potato, green peas and cilantro and Take off the wok from burner.
12. With a paper towel, pat dry the zucchini halves.
13. Stuff the zucchini halves with the veggie mixture.
14. Cover the baking pan and bake in your oven for around 20 minutes.
15. Enjoy hot.

**Nutritional Facts:**
Calories: 169| Fat: 3.2g| Carbs: 32.1g| Protein: 6.5g

## Banana & Tomato Curry

**Serving Portions:** 4| **Preparation Period:** 15 mins.| **Cooking Period:** 7 mins.

**Ingredients Required:**

- 2 tbsp. olive oil
- 2 onions, cut up
- 8cloves garlic, finely cut up
- 1 tbsp. curry powder
- ½ tsp. powdered ginger
- ½ tsp. powdered cumin
- ½ tsp. powdered turmeric
- ½ tsp. powdered cinnamon
- 1 tsp. red chili powder
- Salt and powdered black pepper, as desired
- 2/3 C. fat-free plain Greek yogurt
- 1 (10-oz.) can sugar-free tomato sauce

- 2 large-sized bananas, peel removed and slivered
- 3 tomatoes, cut up
- ¼ C. unsweetened coconut flakes

**Procedure of Cooking:**

1. In a large-sized saucepan, sizzle the oil on burner at around medium heat.
2. Cook the onion for around 4-5 minutes.
3. Put in garlic, curry powder, sugar and spices and sauté for around 1 minute.
4. Put in yogurt and tomato sauce.
5. Cook the mixture until boiling..
6. Blend in bananas.
7. Cook for around 3 minutes.
8. Blend in tomatoes.
9. Cook for around 1-2 minutes.
10. Blend in coconut flakes and immediately take off from burner.
11. Enjoy hot.

**Nutritional Facts:**
Calories: 290| Fat: 15.6g| Carbs: 35.4g| Protein: 6.2g

## Asparagus & Spinach Curry

**Serving Portions:** 4| **Preparation Period:** 15 mins.| **Cooking Period:** 20 mins.

**Ingredients Required:**

- 2 tsp. coconut oil
- 1 small-sized onion, cut up
- 2 cloves garlic, cut up finely
- 1 tbsp. ginger root (fresh), cut up finely
- Salt, as desired
- 3 carrots, peel removed and cut into ¾-inch round slice
- 2 C. asparagus, cut into pieces
- 2 tbsp. green curry paste
- 1 (14-oz.) can coconut milk (unsweetened)
- ½ C. water
- 2 C. fresh baby spinach, roughly cut up
- 1½ tsp. balsamic vinegar

- ½ tsp. red pepper flakes

**Procedure of Cooking:**

1. In a large-sized deep wok, sizzle coconut oil on burner at around medium heat.
2. Cook the onion, garlic, ginger and a pinch of salt for around 5 minutes.
3. Put in carrots and asparagus.
4. Cook for around 3-4 minutes, mixing time to time.
5. Blend in the curry paste.
6. Cook for around 2 minutes, mixing time to time.
7. Put in coconut milk and water.
8. Cook the mixture until boiling.
9. Cook for around 6-10 minutes.
10. Blend in the spinach.
11. Cook for around 2-3 minutes.
12. Blend in vinegar, salt and red pepper flakes and take off from burner.
13. Enjoy hot.

**Nutritional Facts:**
Calories: 249 | Fat: 17.7g | Carbs: 17.5g | Protein: 4g

## Mushrooms & Corn Curry

**Serving Portions:** 4 | **Preparation Period:** 15 mins. | **Cooking Period:** 20 mins.

**Ingredients Required:**

- 2 C. tomatoes, cut up
- 1 green chili, cut up
- 1 tsp. ginger root (fresh), cut up
- ¼ C. cashews
- 2 tbsp. olive oil
- ½ tsp. cumin seeds
- ¼ tsp. powdered coriander
- ¼ tsp. powdered turmeric
- ¼ tsp. red chili powder
- 1½ C. fresh shiitake mushrooms, slivered
- 1½ C. fresh button mushrooms, slivered

- 1 C. frozen corn kernels
- 1¼ C. water
- ¼ C. coconut milk (unsweetened)
- Salt and powdered black pepper, as desired

**Procedure of Cooking:**

1. In a clean food mixer, put in tomatoes, green chili, ginger and cashews and process until a smooth paste forms.
2. In a large-sized saucepan, sizzle the oil on burner at around medium heat.
3. Cook the cumin seeds for around 1 minute.
4. Put in spices and sauté for around 1 minute.
5. Put in tomato paste.
6. Cook for around 5 minutes.
7. Blend in mushrooms, corn, water, coconut milk, salt and pepper.
8. Cook for around 10-12 minutes, mixing time to time.
9. Enjoy hot.

**Nutritional Facts:**
Calories: 208 | Fat: 15.3g | Carbs: 17.4g | Protein: 5.3g

## Ratatouille

**Serving Portions:** 4 | **Preparation Period:** 20 mins. | **Cooking Period:** 45 mins.

**Ingredients Required:**

- 6 oz. homemade tomato paste
- 3 tbsp. olive oil, divided
- ½ onion, cut up
- 3 tbsp. garlic, finely cut up
- Salt and powdered black pepper, as desired
- ¾ C. water
- 1 zucchini, slivered into thin circles
- 1 yellow squash, slivered into circles thinly
- 1 eggplant, slivered into circles thinly

- 2 bell peppers, seeds removed and slivered into circles thinly
- 1 tbsp. thyme (fresh) leaves, finely cut up
- 1 tbsp. lemon juice (fresh)

**Procedure of Cooking:**

1. For preheating: set your oven at 375°F.
2. In a bowl, put in tomato paste, 1 tbsp. of oil, onion, garlic, salt and pepper and blend nicely.
3. Place the tomato paste mixture in the bottom of a 10x10-inch baking pan and spread.
4. Arrange alternating vegetable slices, starting at the outer edge of the baking pan and working concentrically towards the center.
5. Drizzle the vegetables with the remnant oil and sprinkle with salt and pepper, followed by the thyme.
6. Arrange a piece of bakery paper over the vegetables.
7. Bake in your oven for around 45 minutes.
8. Enjoy hot.

**Nutritional Facts:**
Calories: 206 | Fat: 11.4g | Carbs: 26.4g | Protein: 5.4g

---

## Veggie Gumbo

**Serving Portions:** 6 | **Preparation Period:** 15 mins. | **Cooking Period:** 55 mins.

**Ingredients Required:**

- 3 tbsp. olive oil, divided
- 1 medium-sized bell pepper, seeds removed and cut up finely
- 1 medium-sized onion, cut up finely
- 1 clove garlic, finely cut up
- 1 tsp. ginger root (fresh), finely cut up
- 8 oz. mushrooms (fresh), slivered
- ½ of (16-oz.) package frozen okra, thawed and slivered

- 3 cups tomatoes, finely cut up
- 6-oz. homemade tomato paste
- 2 bay leaves
- 1 tsp. thyme (dried)
- ½ tsp. powdered cayenne pepper
- ¼ tsp. red pepper flakes
- Salt and powdered black pepper, as desired
- 2 tbsp. almond flour

**Procedure of Cooking:**

1. In a large-sized saucepan, sizzle 1 tbsp. of oil on burner at around medium heat.
2. Cook the bell pepper, onion and garlic for around 4-5 minutes.
3. Blend in mushrooms, okra, tomatoes, tomato paste, bay leaves, thyme and spices.
4. Cook for around 40 minutes, mixing time to time.
5. Meanwhile, in a frying pan, sizzle remnant oil on burner at around medium heat.
6. Gradually put in flour, mixing all the time to form a smooth mixture.
7. Cook for around 3-5 minutes, mixing all the time.
8. Put in roux in gumbo mixture, mixing all the time.
9. Cook for around 5-10 minutes, mixing time to time.
10. Enjoy hot.

**Nutritional Facts:**
Calories: 177 | Fat: 11g | Carbs: 17.4g | Protein: 5.7g

---

## Curried Veggies Bake

**Serving Portions:** 6 | **Preparation Period:** 15 mins. | **Cooking Period:** 20 mins.

**Ingredients Required:**

- Olive oil baking spray
- 1 medium-sized zucchini, cut up

- 1 medium-sized yellow squash, cut up
- 1 green bell pepper, seeds removed and cubed
- 1 red bell pepper, seeds removed and cubed
- 1 onion, thinly slivered
- 2 tbsp. coconut oil, liquefied
- 2 tsp. curry powder
- Salt and powdered black pepper, as desired
- ¼ C. homemade vegetable broth
- ½ C. low-fat Parmesan cheese, shredded
- ¼ C. cilantro (fresh) leaves, cut up finely

**Procedure of Cooking:**

1. For preheating: set your oven at 375°F.
2. Lightly spray a large-sized baking pan with baking spray.
3. In a large-sized bowl, put in the zucchini and remnant ingredients except for cilantro and Parmesan and blend to incorporate thoroughly.
4. Shift the vegetable mixture into the baking pan.
5. Bake in your oven for around 15-20 minutes.
6. Take off the vegetables from oven and immediately sprinkle with the Parmesan cheese.
7. Decorate with cilantro and enjoy immediately.

**Nutritional Facts:**
Calories: 96| Fat: 6.1g| Carbs: 7.6g| Protein: 4.3g

## Zucchini Gratin

**Serving Portions:** 4| **Preparation Period:** 15 mins.| **Cooking Period:** 35 mins.

**Ingredients Required:**

- 4 tbsp. olive oil, divided
- ¾ C. whole-wheat breadcrumbs

- ½ C. low-fat Parmesan cheese, grated
- 2 medium-sized shallots, thinly slivered
- 2 cloves garlic, finely cut up
- 2 lb. zucchini, cut into ¼-inch pieces crosswise
- 1 tbsp. thyme leaves (fresh)
- 1 tsp. lemon zest, grated finely
- Salt and powdered black pepper, as desired

**Procedure of Cooking:**

1. For preheating: set your oven at 400°F.
2. Lay out a rack in the middle of the oven.
3. In a bowl, add 2 tbsp. of the oil, breadcrumbs and Parmesan cheese and blend to incorporate thoroughly.
4. In an 8-inch cast-iron wok, sizzle the remnant oil on burner at around medium heat.
5. Cook the shallots for around 3-4 minutes, mixing time to time.
6. Blend in the garlic.
7. Cook for around 1 minute.
8. Take off the wok of shallot mixture from burner and blend in the zucchini, thyme, lemon zest, salt and pepper.
9. Then, spread the zucchini mixture into an even layer and sprinkle with the breadcrumbs mixture evenly.
10. Bake in your oven for around 25-30 minutes.
11. Take off the wok of gratin from oven and put it aside for around 5 minutes before enjoying.

**Nutritional Facts:**
Calories: 283| Fat: 18.5g| Carbs: 14.4g| Protein: 8.1g

## Quinoa with Green Beans

**Serving Portions:** 4| **Preparation Period:** 15 mins.| **Cooking Period:** 25 mins.

**Ingredients Required:**

- 3 tbsp. olive oil, divided
- 1 small-sized onion, cut up
- 2 cloves garlic, finely cut up
- 1 C. dried quinoa, rinsed
- Powdered black pepper, as desired
- 1¾ C. homemade vegetable broth
- 1¼ lb. green beans (fresh), cut into pieces
- 2 tbsp. lemon juice (fresh)
- 2 tbsp. cilantro (fresh), cut up

## Procedure of Cooking:

1. In a large-sized saucepan, sizzle 1 tbsp. of the oil on burner at around medium heat.
2. Cook the onion for around 2-3 minutes.
3. Put in garlic and sauté for around 1 minute.
4. Put in quinoa.
5. Cook for around 1 minute, mixing all the time.
6. Blend in the black pepper and broth.
7. Cook the mixture until boiling.
8. Immediately turn the heat at around low.
9. Cook with a cover for around 15 minutes.
10. Take off from burner and put the pan aside with a cover for around 10 minutes.
11. With a fork, fluff the quinoa.
12. Meanwhile, in a saucepan of the boiling water, put in green beans.
13. Cook for around 4-5 minutes.
14. Take off from burner and drain the green beans well.
15. In a large-sized serving bowl, put in quinoa, green beans, lemon juice, remnant oil and black pepper and toss it all to mingle nicely.
16. Decorate with cilantro and enjoy.

## Nutritional Facts:
Calories: 299| Fat: 13.3g g| Carbs: 39.7g| Protein: 8.5g

# Quinoa with Spinach

**Serving Portions:** 4| **Preparation Period:** 15 mins.| **Cooking Period:** 32 mins.

## Ingredients Required:

- 1 tbsp. olive oil
- 1 small-sized onion, finely cut up
- 1 clove garlic, finely cut up
- 1 C. quinoa, rinsed
- 1¼ C. water
- 5 C. fresh baby spinach
- 1 tbsp. lemon zest, grated
- Salt and powdered black pepper, as desired

## Procedure of Cooking:

1. In a large-sized saucepan, sizzle the oil on burner at around medium.
2. Cook the onion and garlic for around 4 minutes.
3. Put in quinoa.
4. Cook for around 1 minute.
5. Put in water.
6. Cook the mixture until boiling.
7. Immediately turn the heat at around low.
8. Cook with a cover for around 20 minutes.
9. Blend in spinach and lemon zest.
10. Cook for around 1-2 minutes.
11. Blend in salt and pepper and enjoy hot.

## Nutritional Facts:

Calories: 204| Fat: 6.3g| Carbs: 30.8g| Protein: 7.4g

# Quinoa & Veggies Bake

**Serving Portions:** 6| **Preparation Period:** 15 mins.| **Cooking Period:** 25 mins.

## Ingredients Required:

- 2 C. Baby Bella mushrooms (fresh)

- 3 tbsp. extra-virgin olive oil, divided
- Salt and powdered black pepper, as desired
- 2 C. cooked quinoa
- 2 C. fresh baby kale
- 2 tbsp. parsley (fresh), cut up

**Procedure of Cooking:**

1. For preheating: set your oven at 425°F.
2. Line a large-sized rimmed baking tray with baking paper.
3. In a bowl, put in mushrooms, 1 tbsp. of oil, salt and pepper and toss it all to mingle nicely.
4. Lay out the mushroom onto the baking tray in a single layer.
5. Roast for around 15-18 minutes, tossing once halfway through.
6. Divide the quinoa, mushrooms, kale and parsley into serving bowls and drizzle with remnant oil.
7. Enjoy immediately.

**Nutritional Facts:**
Calories: 244| Fat: 9.6g| Carbs: 32.8g| Protein: 7.6g

## Lentil Stuffed Zucchini

**Serving Portions:** 8| **Preparation Period:** 15 mins.| **Cooking Period:** 25 mins.

**Ingredients Required:**

- Olive oil baking spray
- ¼ C. olive oil
- 1 clove garlic, cut up
- 4 medium-sized zucchinis, cut in half lengthwise
- Salt and powdered black pepper, as desired
- 1 small-sized onion, cut up finely
- ½ C. canned green lentils, drained and rinsed
- ½ C. dry breadcrumbs
- ½ C. feta cheese, crumbled and divided

**Procedure of Cooking:**

1. For preheating: set your grill to medium-high heat.
2. Spray the grill grate with baking spray.
3. In a small-sized bowl, blend all together the oil and garlic. Put it aside.
4. With a spoon, scrape out the insides of each zucchini half, leaving about ¼-inch thick zucchini shells.
5. Brush each zucchini half with the garlicky oil and then sprinkle with salt and pepper.
6. Then chop the scooped-out zucchini flesh roughly.
7. In a medium-sized wok, sizzle the remnant garlicky oil set on burner at around medium-high heat.
8. Cook the onion and cut up zucchini flesh for around 3-5 minutes.
9. Put in lentils and blend.
10. Cook for around 4-5 minutes, mixing frequently.
11. Shift the lentil mixture into a bowl and put it aside to cool slightly.
12. In the bowl of lentil mixture, put in breadcrumbs, half of the cheese, salt and pepper and blend to incorporate.
13. Stuff each zucchini half with lentil mixture and sprinkle with remnant cheese.
14. Place stuffed zucchini halves onto the grill and cover with the lid.
15. Cook for around 10 minutes.
16. Enjoy immediately.

**Nutritional Facts:**
Calories: 174| Fat: 9.5g| Carbs: 16.7g| Protein: 6.6g

## Lentil Chili

**Serving Portions:** 8| **Preparation Period:** 15 mins.| **Cooking Period:** 2 hrs. 10 mins.

**Ingredients Required:**

- 2 tsp. extra-virgin olive oil
- 1 large-sized onion, cut up

- 2 medium-sized carrots, peel removed and cut up
- 2 celery stalks, cut up
- 1 large-sized bell pepper, seeds removed and cut up
- 2 cloves garlic, finely cut up
- 1 jalapeño pepper, seeds removed and cut up
- 1 tbsp. chipotle chili powder
- 1½ tbsp. powdered coriander
- 1½ tbsp. powdered cumin
- Salt and powdered black pepper, as desired
- 1 lb. red lentils, rinsed
- 2 tbsp. tomato past
- 8 C. homemade vegetable broth
- 4 C. spinach (fresh), torn
- ¼ C. mint leaves (fresh), cut up
- ¼ C. cilantro (fresh), cut up

## Procedure of Cooking:

1. In a large-sized soup pan, sizzle the oil on burner at around medium heat.
2. Cook the onion, carrot and celery for around 5 minutes.
3. Put in garlic, jalapeño pepper and spices and sauté for around 1 minute.
4. Put in tomato paste, lentils and broth.
5. Cook the mixture until boiling.
6. Immediately turn the heat at around low.
7. Cook for around 2 hours.
8. Blend in the spinach.
9. Cook for around 3-4 minutes.
10. Enjoy hot with the decoration of mint and cilantro.

## Nutritional Facts:
Calories: 258 | Fat: 2.2g | Carbs: 45.5g | Protein: 16.3g

## Spicy Lentil Curry

**Serving Portions:** 8 | **Preparation Period:** 10 mins. | **Cooking Period:** 45 mins.

## Ingredients Required:

- 2 C. red lentils, rinsed
- 1 tbsp. olive oil
- 1 large-sized onion, cut up
- 1 tsp. ginger root (fresh), finely cut up
- 1 tsp. garlic, finely cut up
- 2 tbsp. curry paste
- 1 tbsp. curry powder
- 1 tsp. powdered cumin
- 1 tsp. powdered turmeric
- 1 tsp. red chili powder
- Salt and powdered black pepper, as desired
- 2½ C. homemade tomato puree

## Procedure of Cooking:

1. In a large-sized saucepan of water, put in lentils on burner at around high heat.
2. Cook the mixture until boiling.
3. Immediately turn the heat at around medium-low.
4. Cook with a cover for around 15-20 minutes.
5. Drain the lentils well.
6. In a large-sized wok, sizzle the oil on burner at around medium heat.
7. Cook the onion for around 10 minutes.
8. Meanwhile, in a bowl, blend all together ginger, garlic, spices, salt and pepper.
9. Put in spice mixture into the wok with onions and blend to incorporate.
10. Cook for around 1-2 minutes, mixing all the time.
11. Blend in tomato puree.
12. Cook for around 1 minute.
13. Shift the mixture into the pan with the lentils and blend to incorporate.
14. Enjoy hot.

## Nutritional Facts:
Calories: 192 | Fat: 2.6g | Carbs: 32.5g | Protein: 12.1g

# Lentils with Spinach

**Serving Portions:** 6 | **Preparation Period:** 15 mins. | **Cooking Period:** 35 mins.

**Ingredients Required:**

- 3½ C. water
- 1½ C. red lentils, soaked for 20 minutes and drained
- ½ tsp. red chili powder
- ½ tsp. powdered turmeric
- Salt, as desired
- 1 lb. spinach (fresh), cut up
- 2 tbsp. coconut oil
- 1 onion, cut up
- 1 tsp. mustard seeds
- 1 tsp. powdered cumin
- ½ C. coconut milk (unsweetened)
- 1 tsp. garam masala powder

**Procedure of Cooking:**

1. In a large-sized saucepan, put in water, lentils, red chili powder, turmeric and salt on burner at around high heat.
2. Cook the mixture until boiling.
3. Immediately turn the heat at around low.
4. Cook with a cover for around 15 minutes.
5. Blend in spinach.
6. Cook for around 5 minutes.
7. In a frying pan, sizzle coconut oil on burner at around medium heat.
8. Cook the onion, mustard seeds and cumin and sauté for around 4-5 minutes.
9. Shift the onion mixture into the pan with the lentils and blend to incorporate.
10. Blend in coconut milk and garam masala.
11. Cook for around 3-5 minutes.
12. Enjoy hot.

**Nutritional Facts:**
Calories: 268 | Fat: 8.4g | Carbs: 34.4g | Protein: 15.2g

# Barley Pilaf

**Serving Portions:** 4 | **Preparation Period:** 15 mins. | **Cooking Period:** 1 hr. 5 mins.

**Ingredients Required:**

- ½ C. pearl barley
- 1 C. homemade vegetable broth
- 2 tbsp. vegetable oil, divided
- 2 cloves garlic, finely cut up
- ½ C. onion, cut up
- ½ C. green olives, slivered
- 1 C. bell pepper, seeds removed and cut up
- 2 tbsp. cilantro (fresh), cut up
- 2 tbsp. mint leaves (fresh), cut up

**Procedure of Cooking:**

1. In a saucepan, put in barley and broth on burner at around medium-high heat.
2. Cook the mixture until boiling.
3. Immediately turn the heat at around low.
4. Cook with a cover for around 45 minutes.
5. In a large-sized wok, sizzle 1 tbsp. of the oil on burner at around medium-high heat.
6. Cook the garlic for around 30 seconds.
7. Blend in the cooked barley.
8. Cook for around 3 minutes.
9. Take off from burner and put it aside
10. In another wok, sizzle the remnant oil on burner at around medium heat.
11. Cook the onion for around 7 minutes.
12. Put in olives and bell pepper and stir-fry for around 3 minutes.
13. Blend in remnant ingredients except.
14. Cook for around 3 minutes.
15. Blend in the barley mixture.
16. Cook for around 3 minutes.
17. Enjoy hot with the decoration of walnuts.

**Nutritional Facts:**
Calories: 204| Fat: 10.1g| Carbs: 25.3g|
Protein: 4.8g

---

## Brown Rice & Mushroom Bake

**Serving Portions:** 2| **Preparation Period:** 15
mins.| **Cooking Period:** 1 hr.

**Ingredients Required:**

- 1 tsp. extra-virgin olive oil
- 1 red onion, slivered thinly
- 1½ tsp. powdered turmeric
- 9 oz. brown mushrooms, slivered
- 1 tsp. raisins
- ½ C. brown rice, rinsed
- 1¼ C. homemade vegetable broth
- ¼ C. cilantro (fresh), cut up
- ½ tbsp. pine nuts, toasted
- 1 tbsp. lemon juice (fresh)
- Salt and powdered black pepper, as
  desired

**Procedure of Cooking:**

1. For preheating: set your oven at 400°F.
2. In an ovenproof saucepan, sizzle the oil
   on burner at around medium heat.
3. Cook the onion and turmeric for
   around 3 minutes.
4. Put in mushrooms and stir-fry for
   around 2 minutes.
5. Blend in raisins, rice and broth and
   shift into oven.
6. Bake in your oven for around 45-55
   minutes.
7. Take off the pan of rice mixture from
   burner and blend in remnant
   ingredients.
8. Enjoy hot.

**Nutritional Facts:**
Calories: 201| Fat: 5g| Carbs: 33.7g| Protein:
6.7g

# Sides Recipes

## Glazed Baby Carrots

**Serving Portions:** 4 | **Preparation Period:** 15 mins. | **Cooking Period:** 15 mins.

**Ingredients Required:**

- 2 C. water
- 1 lb. baby carrots
- 3 tbsp. maple syrup
- 1 tbsp. coconut oil
- 1 tsp. powdered cinnamon
- Salt, as desired
- 1 tbsp. lemon juice (fresh)
- 2 tbsp. parsley (fresh), cut up
- Powdered black pepper, as desired
- 1 tbsp. parsley (fresh), finely cut up

**Procedure of Cooking:**

1. In a medium-sized saucepan, put in water on burner at around medium-high heat.
2. Cook the water until boiling.
3. Put in carrots and blend.
4. Again, cook the mixture until boiling.
5. Immediately turn the heat at around medium.
6. Cook for around 6-8 minutes.
7. Drain the carrots thoroughly
8. In a wok, put in maple syrup, coconut oil, lemon juice, salt and pepper.
9. Cook for around 5 minutes, mixing all the time.
10. Blend in the parsley and enjoy warm.

**Nutritional Facts:**
Calories: 118 | Fat: 3.5g | Carbs: 21.9g | Protein: 1g

## Garlicky Spinach

**Serving Portions:** 4 | **Preparation Period:** 10 mins. | **Cooking Period:** 7 mins.

**Ingredients Required:**

- 1 tbsp. olive oil
- 6 cloves garlic, slivered thinly
- 2 (10-oz.) packages spinach (fresh)
- ½ tsp. powdered turmeric
- ½ tsp. powdered cumin
- 1 tbsp. lemon juice (fresh)
- Salt and powdered black pepper, as desired

**Procedure of Cooking:**

1. In a large-sized wok, sizzle the oil on burner at around medium heat.
2. Cook the garlic for around 1 minute.
3. Put in spinach and spices.
4. Cook for around 5 minutes.
5. Blend in lemon juice, salt and pepper and take off from burner.
6. Enjoy hot.

**Nutritional Facts:**
Calories: 72 | Fat: 4.2g | Carbs: 7g | Protein: 4.4g

## Kale with Cranberries & Pine Nuts

**Serving Portions:** 6 | **Preparation Period:** 15 mins. | **Cooking Period:** 14 mins.

**Ingredients Required:**

- 2 lb. kale (fresh), tough ribs removed and cut up
- 3 tbsp. extra-virgin olive oil
- 1 tbsp. garlic, finely cut up
- ½ C. dried unsweetened cranberries

- Salt and powdered black pepper, as desired
- 1/3 C. pine nuts

**Procedure of Cooking:**

1. In a large-sized saucepan of boiling salted water, cook the kale for around 5-7 minutes.
2. In a colander, drain the kale and immediately transfer into an ice bath.
3. Drain the kale and put it aside.
4. In a wok, sizzle the oil on burner at around medium heat.
5. Cook the garlic for around 1 minute.
6. Put in kale, cranberries, salt and pepper.
7. Cook for around 4-6 minutes, tossing frequently with tongs.
8. Blend in the pine nuts and enjoy hot.

**Nutritional Facts:**
Calories: 196| Fat: 12.2g| Carbs: 19.3g| Protein: 5.6g

## Lemony Asparagus

**Serving Portions:** 4| **Preparation Period:** 10 mins.| **Cooking Period:** 7 mins.

**Ingredients Required:**

- 1 lb. asparagus
- 2 tbsp. extra-virgin olive oil
- 1 tbsp. lemon juice (fresh)
- 1 pinch of salt
- Powdered black pepper, as desired

**Procedure of Cooking:**

1. In a saucepan of boiling water, lay out a steamer basket.
2. Place the asparagus in steamer basket and steam with a cover for around 5-7 minutes.
3. Drain the asparagus thoroughly and shift into a bowl.

4. Put in oil, lemon juice, salt and pepper and toss it all to mingle nicely.
5. Enjoy immediately.

**Nutritional Facts:**
Calories: 84| Fat: 7.2g| Carbs: 4.5g| Protein: 2.5g

## Gingered Broccoli

**Serving Portions:** 2
| **Preparation Period:** 10 mins.
| **Cooking Period:** 8 mins.

**Ingredients Required:**

- 1 tbsp. olive oil
- 2 cloves garlic, finely cut up
- 1 tsp. ginger root (fresh), finely cut up
- 2 C. broccoli florets
- 2 tbsp. water
- Salt and powdered black pepper, as desired

**Procedure of Cooking:**

1. In a large-sized wok, sizzle the oil on burner at around medium heat.
2. Cook the garlic and ginger for around 1 minute.
3. Put in broccoli and stir-fry for 2 minutes.
4. Blend in water, salt and black pepper and stir-fry for 4-5 minutes.
5. Enjoy hot.

**Nutritional Facts:**
Calories: 99| Fat: 7.4g| Carbs: 7.7g| Protein: 2.8g

## Lemony Mushrooms

**Serving Portions:** 2| **Preparation Period:** 10 mins.| **Cooking Period:** 15 mins.

**Ingredients Required:**

- 2 tbsp. olive oil
- 2-3 tbsp. red onion, finely cut up
- ½ tsp. garlic, finely cut up
- 12 oz. mushrooms (fresh), slivered
- 1 tbsp. parsley (fresh)
- 2 tsp. lemon juice (fresh)
- Salt and powdered black pepper, as desired

**Procedure of Cooking:**

1. In a wok, sizzle the oil on burner at around medium heat.
2. Cook the onion and garlic for 3-4 minutes.
3. Put in mushrooms and blend.
4. Cook for 8-10 minutes.
5. Blend in the parsley, lemon juice, salt and pepper and take off from burner.
6. Enjoy hot.

**Nutritional Facts:**
Calories: 163| Fat: 14.6g| Carbs: 7g| Protein: 5.6g

## Lemony Zoodles

**Serving Portions:** 8| **Preparation Period:** 15 mins.| **Cooking Period:** 8 mins.

**Ingredients Required:**

- 6 zucchinis, spiralized with Blade C
- Salt, as desired
- 3 tbsp. olive oil
- 1 clove garlic, finely cut up
- 2 tbsp. lemon juice (fresh)
- 2 tbsp. parsley (fresh), cut up
- Powdered black pepper, as desired

**Procedure of Cooking:**

1. In a large-sized bowl, put in zucchini noodles and salt and toss it all to mingle nicely.

2. Shift the zucchini noodles into a large-sized colander and put it aside or at least 30 minutes to drain.
3. In a saucepan of boiling water, put in zucchini noodles.
4. Cook for around 1 minute.
5. Drain the zucchini noodles and rinse them.
6. In a large-sized wok, sizzle oi on burner at around medium-high heat.
7. Cook the garlic for around 1 minute.
8. Put in zucchini noodles.
9. Cook for around 4-5 minutes.
10. Blend in salt and pepper and immediately take off from burner.
11. Enjoy immediately.

**Nutritional Facts:**
Calories: 70| Fat: 5.6g| Carbs: 5.2g| Protein: 1.9g

## Green Beans with Cherry Tomatoes

**Serving Portions:** 8| **Preparation Period:** 15 mins.| **Cooking Period:** 40 mins.

**Ingredients Required:**

- 3-4 cloves garlic, cut up
- 1 tsp. fresh lemon peel, grated freshly
- 2 tsp. olive oil
- 1 tsp. powdered cumin
- Salt and powdered white pepper, as desired
- 4 C. cherry tomatoes
- 1½ lb. green beans (fresh)

**Procedure of Cooking:**

1. For preheating: set your oven at 350°F.
2. In a large-sized bowl, blend all together garlic, lemon peel, oil, cumin, salt and white pepper.
3. Put in cherry tomatoes and toss it all to mingle nicely.
4. Shift the tomato mixture into a roasting pan.
5. Roast in your oven for around 35-40 minutes, mixing once halfway through.

6. Meanwhile in a saucepan of boiling water, put in steamer basket.
7. Place the green beans in the steamer basket and steam, covered for around 7-8 minutes.
8. Drain the green beans well and shift into a large-sized bowl.
9. Take off the roasting pan from oven.
10. Place the tomatoes into the bowl of green beans stir to blend.
11. Enjoy immediately.

**Nutritional Facts:**
Calories: 55| Fat: 1.5g| Carbs: 10.1g| Protein: 2.5g

## Green Beans with Mushrooms

**Serving Portions:** 2| **Preparation Period:** 15 mins.| **Cooking Period:** 20 mins.

**Ingredients Required:**

- 2 tbsp. olive oil
- 2 tbsp. onion, finely cut up
- ½ tsp. garlic, finely cut up
- 1 (8-oz.) package white mushrooms, slivered
- 1 C. frozen green beans
- Salt and powdered black pepper, as desired
- 2 tbsp. low-fat Parmesan cheese, grated

**Procedure of Cooking:**

1. In a medium-sized wok, sizzle the oil on burner at around medium heat.
2. Cook the onion and garlic for around 2-3 minutes.
3. Put in mushrooms and blend.
4. Cook for around 6-7 minutes.
5. Blend in the green beans.
6. Cook for around 5-10 minutes.

7. Enjoy hot with the decoration of parmesan cheese.

**Nutritional Facts:**
Calories: 166| Fat: 13.1g| Carbs: 8.8g| Protein: 6.8g

## Yellow Squash with Bell Peppers

**Serving Portions:** 4| **Preparation Period:** 15 mins.| **Cooking Period:** 10 mins.

**Ingredients Required:**

- 1 tbsp. olive oil
- ½ C. onion, slivered
- 1 C. bell pepper, seeds removed and julienned
- 3 C. yellow squash, slivered
- 1½ tsp. garlic, finely cut up
- ¼ C. water
- Salt and powdered black pepper, as desired

**Procedure of Cooking:**

1. In a large-sized wok, sizzle the oil on burner at around medium-high heat.
2. Cook the onion, bell peppers and squash for around 4-5 minutes.
3. Put in garlic and sauté for around 1 minute.
4. Blend in remnant ingredients and immediately turn the heat at around medium.
5. Cook for around 3-4 minutes, mixing time to time.
6. Enjoy hot.

**Nutritional Facts:**
Calories: 61| Fat: 3.8g| Carbs: 6.8g| Protein: 1.6g

# Snacks Recipes

## Apple Chips

**Serving Portions:** 6 | **Preparation Period:** 10 mins. | **Cooking Period:** 2 hrs.

**Ingredients Required:**

- 2 tbsp. powdered cinnamon
- 1 tbsp. powdered ginger
- 1½ tsp. powdered cloves
- 1½ tsp. powdered nutmeg
- 3 Fuji apples, slivered thinly in rounds

**Procedure of Cooking:**

1. For preheating: set your oven at 200°F.
2. Lay out bakery paper onto a large-sized baking tray.
3. In a bowl, blend all together all spices.
4. Lay out the apple slices into prepared baking tray and sprinkle with spice mixture.
5. Bake in your oven for around 1 hour.
6. Change the side and again sprinkle with spice mixture.
7. Bake in your oven for around 1 hour.
8. Enjoy warm.

**Nutritional Facts:**
Calories: 71 | Fat: 0.6g | Carbs: 18.5g | Protein: 0.5g

## Spinach Chips

**Serving Portions:** 2 | **Preparation Period:** 10 mins. | **Cooking Period:** 8 mins.

**Ingredients Required:**

- 4 C. spinach (fresh) leaves
- 1-2 tsp. extra-virgin olive oil
- Salt, as desired
- ½ tsp. Italian seasoning

**Procedure of Cooking:**

1. For preheating: set your oven at 325°F.
2. Lay out bakery paper onto a large-sized baking tray.
3. In a large-sized bowl, put in spinach leaves and drizzle with oil.
4. With your hands, rub the spinach leaves until all the leaves are coated with oil.
5. Shift the leaves 0nto the baking tray and spread in a single layer.
6. Sprinkle the spinach leaves with salt and Italian seasoning.
7. Bake in your oven for around 8 minutes.
8. Take off the baking tray of chips from oven and put it aside for around 5 minutes before enjoying.

**Nutritional Facts:**
Calories: 37 | Fat: 2.9g | Carbs: 2.3g | Protein: 1.7g

## Cinnamon Popcorn

**Serving Portions:** 3 | **Preparation Period:** 10 mins. | **Cooking Period:** 5 mins.

**Ingredients Required:**

- 2 tbsp. coconut oil
- ¾ C. popping corn
- ¼ tsp. powdered cinnamon

**Procedure of Cooking:**

1. In a saucepan, sizzle coconut oil on medium-high heat.
2. Put in popping corn and cover the pan tightly.
3. Cook for around 1-2 minutes, shaking the pan time to time.
4. Take off the saucepan from burner and shift into a large-sized heatproof bowl.

5. Put in cinnamon and blend to incorporate thoroughly.
6. Enjoy immediately

**Nutritional Facts:**
Calories: 112| Fat: 9.5g| Carbs: 7.4g| Protein: 1.3g

## Sweet & Spicy Cashews

**Serving Portions:** 8| **Preparation Period:** 10 mins.| **Cooking Period:** 20 mins.

**Ingredients Required:**

- 2 C. cashews
- 2 tsp. raw honey
- 1½ tsp. smoked paprika
- ½ tsp. chili flakes
- Salt, as desired
- 1 tbsp. lemon juice (fresh)
- 1 tsp. olive oil

**Procedure of Cooking:**

1. For preheating: set your oven at 350°F.
2. Lay out bakery paper into a baking pan.
3. In a bowl, put in cashews and remnant ingredients and toss it all to mingle nicely.
4. Shift the cashew mixture into baking pan.
5. Roast for around 20 minutes, changing the side once after 10 minutes.
6. Take off from oven and put it aside to cool thoroughly before enjoying.

**Nutritional Facts:**
Calories: 209| Fat: 16.5g| Carbs: 12.9g| Protein: 5.3g

## Apple Cookies

**Serving Portions:** 20 portions| **Preparation Period:** 15 mins.| **Cooking Period:** 12 mins.

**Ingredients Required:**

- Olive oil baking spray
- 2 tsp. chia seeds
- ¼ C. warm water
- 2 C. gluten-free quick oats, divided
- ½ tsp. baking soda
- ½ tsp. powdered cinnamon
- ¼ tsp. powdered nutmeg
- ¼ tsp. powdered ginger
- 1 pinch of powdered cloves
- ¼ C. raisins
- 1 large-sized apple, peel removed, cored and cut up
- 4 Medjool dates, pitted and cut up
- 1 tsp. apple cider vinegar
- 2 tbsp. water

**Procedure of Cooking:**

1. For preheating: set your oven at 375°F.
2. Lay out bakery paper onto a large-sized cookie tray and then spray it with baking spray.
3. In a bowl, soak the chia seeds in warm water and put it aside until thickened.
4. In a food mixer, put in 1 C. of oats and process until finely ground.
5. Shift the ground oats in a large-sized mixing bowl.
6. Put in remnant oats and remnant ingredients and process to form a smooth mixture.
7. Shift the apple mixture into the bowl with oat mixture and blend to incorporate thoroughly.
8. Put in chia seeds mixture and blend to incorporate.
9. Spoon the mixture onto prepared cookie tray about 1-inch apart.
10. With your hands, flatten each cookie slightly.
11. Bake in your oven for around 12 minutes.
12. Take off from oven and place the cookie tray onto a counter to cool for around 5 minutes.
13. Then take off the cookies from tray and shift onto a platter to cool before enjoying.

**Nutritional Facts:**
Calories: 60| Fat: 0.7g| Carbs: 12g| Protein: 1.6g

## Seeds Crackers

**Serving Portions:** 10| **Preparation Period:** 15 mins.| **Cooking Period:** 12 hrs.

**Ingredients Required:**

- 2 C. water
- 1 C. sunflower seeds
- 1 C. flaxseeds
- 1 tbsp. ginger root (fresh), cut up
- 1 tsp. unsweetened applesauce
- ¼ C. lemon juice (fresh)
- 1 tsp. powdered turmeric
- 1 pinch of salt

**Procedure of Cooking:**

1. In a bowl, put in water, sunflower seeds and flaxseeds and soak all the night.
2. Drain the seeds.
3. In a food mixer, put in soaked seeds and remnant ingredients and process to incorporate thoroughly.
4. Set dehydrator at 115°F.
5. Line a dehydrator tray with unbleached bakery paper.
6. Place the mixture onto prepared dehydrator tray.
7. With a knife, score the size of crackers.
8. Dehydrate for around 12 hours.

**Nutritional Facts:**
Calories: 90| Fat: 6g| Carbs: 4.8g| Protein: 3.2g

## Blueberry Energy Bites

**Serving Portions:** 8| **Preparation Period:** 15 mins.

**Ingredients Required:**

- 1 scoop unsweetened| Protein: powder

- ½ C. coconut flour, sifted
- 1-2 tbsp. Erythritol
- ¼ tsp. powdered cinnamon
- 1 pinch of salt
- ¼ C. dried blueberries
- ½-1 C. almond milk (unsweetened)

**Procedure of Cooking:**

1. Lay out bakery paper onto a large-sized cookie tray. Put it aside.
2. In a large-sized bowl, blend all together and remnant ingredients except almond milk.
3. Slowly, put in desired amount of almond milk and mix until a dough is formed.
4. Immediately shape the mixture into balls.
5. Lay out the balls onto prepared baking tray.
6. Shift into your refrigerator to set for around 30 minutes before enjoying.

**Nutritional Facts:**
Calories: 50| Fat: 1.1g| Carbs: 5.9g| Protein: 4.3g

## Tomato Bruschetta

**Serving Portions:** 6| **Preparation Period:** 15 mins.| **Cooking Period:** 4 mins.

**Ingredients Required:**

- ½ of whole-grain baguette, cut into 6 (½-inch-thick) slices diagonally
- 3 tomatoes, cut up
- ½ C. fennel, cut up
- 2 cloves garlic, finely cut up
- 1 tbsp. parsley (fresh), cut up
- 1 tbsp. basil (fresh), cut up
- 2 tsp. balsamic vinegar
- 1 tsp. olive oil
- Salt and powdered black pepper, as desired

**Procedure of Cooking:**

1. For preheating: set your oven at broiler.
2. Arrange a rack in the top portion of the oven.
3. Lay out the bread slices onto a baking tray in a single layer.
4. Broil for around 2 minutes from both sides.
5. Meanwhile in a bowl, put in remnant ingredients and toss it all to mingle nicely.
6. Place the tomato mixture on each toasted bread slice and enjoy immediately.

**Nutritional Facts:**
Calories: 102 | Fat: 2.4g | Carbs: 16.3g | Protein: 3.7g

## Fruity Salsa

**Serving Portions:** 8 | **Preparation Period:** 15 mins.

**Ingredients Required:**

- 8 oz. fresh pineapple, cut up
- 2 large-sized mangoes, peel removed, pitted and cut up
- ½ C. red onion, cut up
- 1 tbsp. ginger root (fresh), finely grated
- ¼ C. cilantro (fresh), cut up
- 1 tsp. red pepper flakes
- 3 tbsp. apple cider vinegar

**Procedure of Cooking:**

1. In a large-sized serving bowl, put in pineapple and remnant ingredients and gently stir to combine.
2. Enjoy immediately.

**Nutritional Facts:**
Calories: 72 | Fat: 0.4g | Carbs: 17.7g | Protein: 1g

## Strawberry & Veggie Gazpacho

**Serving Portions:** 4 | **Preparation Period:** 15 mins.

**Ingredients Required:**

- 1 ½ lb. strawberries (fresh), slivered
- ½ C. red bell pepper, seeds removed and cut up
- 1 small-sized cucumber, peel, seeds removed and cut up
- ¼ C. onion, cut up
- ¼ C. basil leaves (fresh)
- 1 clove garlic, cut up
- ¼ of small-sized jalapeño pepper, seeds removed and cut up
- 1 tbsp. olive oil
- 2 tbsp. apple cider vinegar

**Procedure of Cooking:**

1. In a high-power mixer, put in 1 ½ lb. of the strawberries and remnant ingredients and process to form a smooth mixture.
2. Shift the gazpacho into a large-sized serving bowl.
3. Cover the bowl of gazpacho and shift into your refrigerator for around 4 hours before enjoying.

**Nutritional Facts:**
Calories: 106 | Fat: 4.2g | Carbs: 17.8g | Protein: 1.9g

# Smoothies Recipes

## Coffee Smoothie

**Serving Portions:** 2 | **Preparation Period:** 10 minutes

**Ingredients Required:**

- 1 large-sized frozen banana, peel removed and slivered
- 1 scoop unsweetened | Protein: powder
- 1 C. cold brewed coffee
- 1 C. almond milk (unsweetened)

**Procedure of Cooking:**

1. In a high-power processor, put in banana and remnant ingredients and process to form creamy mixture.
2. Enjoy immediately.

**Nutritional Facts:**
Calories: 132 | Fat: 2.5g | Carbs: 14.5g | Protein: 14g

## Cranberry Smoothie

**Serving Portions:** 2 | **Preparation Period:** 10 minutes

**Ingredients Required:**

- 1 C. cranberries (fresh)
- 1½ scoops unsweetened protein powder
- 1 tsp. vanilla extract
- 1 tbsp. honey
- 1¼ C. almond milk (unsweetened)
- ½ C. ice cubes

**Procedure of Cooking:**

1. In a high-power processor, put in cranberries and remnant ingredients and process to form creamy mixture.
2. Enjoy immediately.

**Nutritional Facts:**
Calories: 148 | Fat: 3g | Carbs: 7.5g | Protein: 19.6g

## Strawberry & Beet Smoothie

**Serving Portions:** 2 | **Preparation Period:** 10 minutes

**Ingredients Required:**

- ¾ C. raw red beets, cut up
- 1 C. frozen strawberries
- 1 tbsp. honey
- 1½ C. almond milk (unsweetened)
- ½ C. ice cubes

**Procedure of Cooking:**

1. In a high-power processor, put in beets and remnant ingredients and process to form creamy mixture.
2. Enjoy immediately.

**Nutritional Facts:**
Calories: 81 | Fat: 3g | Carbs: 14.4g | Protein: 2.3g

## Cherry Smoothie

**Serving Portions:** 2 | **Preparation Period:** 10 minutes

**Ingredients Required:**

- 1 C. cherries (fresh)
- 1 pinch of powdered cinnamon
- 1 tbsp. maple syrup
- 1½ C. almond milk (unsweetened)
- ½ C. ice cubes

**Procedure of Cooking:**

1. In a high-power processor, put in cherries and remnant ingredients and process to form creamy mixture.

2. Enjoy immediately.

**Nutritional Facts:**
Calories: 80 | Fat: 2.6g | Carbs: 14.6g | Protein: 1.8g

## Carrot & Tomato Smoothie

**Serving Portions:** 2 | **Preparation Period:** 10 minutes

**Ingredients Required:**

- 4 medium-sized tomatoes
- 1 large-sized carrot, peel removed and cut up
- 1 celery stalk, cut up
- 1 pinch of salt
- ¼ tsp. powdered black pepper
- 2 tsp. lemon juice (fresh)
- 1 C. ice cubes

**Procedure of Cooking:**

1. In a high-power processor, put in tomatoes and remnant ingredients and process to form creamy mixture.
2. Enjoy immediately.

**Nutritional Facts:**
Calories: 62 | Fat: 0.6g | Carbs: 13.6g | Protein: 2.6g

## Avocado Chia Seed Smoothie

**Serving Portions:** 2 | **Preparation Period:** 10 minutes

**Ingredients Required:**

- 1 small-sized avocado, peel removed, pitted and cut up
- 1 scoop unflavored collagen powder
- 1 tbsp. chia seeds
- 1½ C. almond milk (unsweetened)
- ½ C. ice cubes

**Procedure of Cooking:**

1. In a high-power processor, put in avocado and remnant ingredients and process to form creamy mixture.
2. Enjoy immediately.

**Nutritional Facts:**
Calories: 215 | Fat: 14.9g | Carbs: 7.9g | Protein: 16.2g

## Green Hemp Smoothie

**Serving Portions:** 2 | **Preparation Period:** 10 minutes

**Ingredients Required:**

- 1 tbsp. raw hemp seeds, shelled
- 2 C. fresh baby spinach
- ½ of avocado, peel removed, pitted and cut up
- 1 tbsp. maple syrup
- ¼ tsp. powdered cinnamon
- 2 C. chilled water

**Procedure of Cooking:**

1. In a high-power processor, put in hempseeds and remnant ingredients and process to form creamy mixture.
2. Enjoy immediately.

**Nutritional Facts:**
Calories: 140 | Fat: 14.3g | Carbs: 6g | Protein: 3.5g

## Coconut Green Smoothie

**Serving Portions:** 2 | **Preparation Period:** 10 minutes

**Ingredients Required:**

- 2 C. spinach (fresh)
- 1 (1-inch) piece ginger root (fresh), peel removed
- ¼ C. unsweetened ground coconut
- 1/8 tsp. salt
- 1½ C. almond milk (unsweetened)
- 1 C. ice

**Procedure of Cooking:**

1. In a high-power processor, put in spinach and remnant ingredients and process to form creamy mixture.
2. Enjoy immediately.

**Nutritional Facts:**
Calories: 79| Fat: 6.2g| Carbs: 5.3g| Protein: 2.5g

## Nutty Spinach Smoothie

**Serving Portions:** 2 | **Preparation Period:** 10 minutes

**Ingredients Required:**

- 2 C. spinach (fresh)
- 2 tbsp. almonds
- 2 tbsp. walnuts
- 2 scoops unsweetened whey protein
- 1 tbsp. psyllium seeds
- 1 tbsp. honey
- 1½ C. almond milk (unsweetened)

**Procedure of Cooking:**

1. In a high-power processor, put in spinach and remnant ingredients and process to form creamy mixture.

2. Enjoy immediately.

**Nutritional Facts:**
Calories: 236| Fat: 11.9g| Carbs: 10.8g| Protein: 28g

## Lettuce & Spinach Smoothie

**Serving Portions:** 2 | **Preparation Period:** 10 minutes

**Ingredients Required:**

- 2 C. romaine lettuce, cut up
- 2 C. fresh baby spinach
- ¼ C. mint leaves (fresh)
- 2 tbsp. lemon juice (fresh)
- 1-2 tbsp. maple syrup
- 1½ C. filtered water
- ½ C. ice cubes

**Procedure of Cooking:**

1. In a high-power processor, put in lettuce and remnant ingredients and process to form creamy mixture.
2. Enjoy immediately.

**Nutritional Facts:**
Calories: 23| Fat: 0.4g| Carbs: 7g| Protein: 1.6g

# Drinks Recipes

## Citrus Detox Water

**Serving Portion:** 3 | **Preparation Period:** 10 mins.

**Ingredients Required:**

- 1 orange, slivered
- 1 lime, slivered
- 1 lemon, slivered
- ½ of cucumber, slivered
- 2 tbsp. mint leaves (fresh)
- 6 C. water

**Procedure of Cooking:**

1. In a large-sized glass jar, put in fruit, cucumber and mint leaves and pour water on top.
2. Cover the jar with a lid and shift into your refrigerator for around 2-4 hours before enjoying.

**Nutritional Facts:**
Calories: 41 | Fat: 0.2g | Carbs: 10.4g | Protein: 1.1g

## Strawberry Detox Water

**Serving Portion:** 6 | **Preparation Period:** 10 mins. | **Cooking Period:** 10 mins.

**Ingredients Required:**

- 1 C. strawberries (fresh), slivered
- 1 lemon, slivered
- 1 tbsp. mint leaves (fresh)
- 6 C. water

**Procedure of Cooking:**

1. In a large-sized glass jar, put in strawberry, lemon and mint leaves and pour water on top.

2. Cover the jar with a lid and shift into your refrigerator for around 2-4 hours before enjoying.

**Nutritional Facts:**
Calories: 18 | Fat: 0.2g | Carbs: 4.3g | Protein: 0.4g

## Lemon Iced Tea

**Serving Portion:** 6 | **Preparation Period:** 10 mins. | **Cooking Period:** 5 mins.

**Ingredients Required:**

- 6 C. water
- ¼ C. lemon juice (fresh)
- 5 thyme (fresh) sprigs
- 1 cinnamon stick
- 3 black tea bags
- 6 tsp. maple syrup

**Procedure of Cooking:**

1. In a large-sized saucepan, put in water, lemon juice, thyme, lemon zest and cinnamon on burner at around medium-high heat.
2. Cook the mixture until boiling.
3. Take off the saucepan from burner and put in tea bags and maple syrup.
4. Cover the pan and put it aside for 15 minutes to steep.
5. Remove tea bags and let the tea cool for around an hour.
6. Through a fine mesh strainer, strain the tea mixture into a pitcher.
7. Shift into your refrigerator to chill before enjoying.

**Nutritional Facts:**
Calories: 4 | Fat: 0.1g | Carbs: 0.5g | Protein: 0.1g

# Cranberry Ice Tea

**Serving Portion:** 7 portions | **Preparation Period:** 10 mins.

**Ingredients Required:**

- 1¼ C. boiling water
- 2 dandelion tea bags
- 5 C. cold water
- 1 C. water kefir
- ½ C. unsweetened cranberry juice
- 6 drops grapefruit oil
- 6 drops lemon oil

**Procedure of Cooking:**

1. In a large-sized glass pitcher, put in boiling water and tea bags and brew, covered for around 8-10 minutes.
2. Discard the tea bags and mix in remnant ingredients.
3. Shift into your refrigerator to chill thoroughly before enjoying.

**Nutritional Facts:**
Calories: 13 | Fat: 0.1g | Carbs: 3.7g | Protein: 0g

# Lemonade

**Serving Portion:** 4 | **Preparation Period:** 10 mins.

**Ingredients Required:**

- ¾ C. lemon juice (fresh)
- 2-3 tbsp. maple syrup
- 3½ C. cold water
- Ice cubes, as desired

**Procedure of Cooking:**

1. In a large-sized pitcher, blend all together the lemon juice and maple syrup.
2. Put in water and fill the pitcher with ice.
3. Enjoy chilled.

**Nutritional Facts:**
Calories: 11 | Fat: 0.4g | Carbs: 1g | Protein: 0.4g

# Chilled Green Tea

**Serving Portion:** 2 | **Preparation Period:** 10 mins.

**Ingredients Required:**

- 2½ C. boiling water
- 1 C. mint leaves (fresh)
- 4 green tea bags
- 2 tsp. raw honey

**Procedure of Cooking:**

- In a pitcher, blend all together water, mint and tea bags.
- Cover and steep for around 5 minutes.
- Shift into your refrigerator for at least 3 hours.
- Discard the tea bags and divide the tea in serving glasses.
- Blend in honey and enjoy.

**Nutritional Facts:**
Calories: 41 | Fat: 0.3g | Carbs: 9.6g | Protein: 1.5g

# Lemon & Ginger Tea

**Serving Portion:** 4 | **Preparation Period:** 10 mins. | **Cooking Period:** 5 mins.

**Ingredients Required:**

- 6 C. water
- ½ of lemon, seeds removed and roughly cut up
- 1 (1-inch) piece ginger root (fresh), cut up
- 2 tbsp. maple syrup
- 1 pinch of powdered turmeric
- 1 pinch of powdered cinnamon

**Procedure of Cooking:**

1. In a saucepan, put in water and remnant ingredients on burner at around medium-high heat.
2. Cook the mixture until boiling.
3. Immediately turn the heat at around medium-low.
4. Cook for around 10-12 minutes.
5. Strain into C. and enjoy hot.

**Nutritional Facts:**
Calories: 29| Fat: 0.1g| Carbs: 7.3g| Protein: 0.1g

## Spiced Ginger Tea

**Serving Portion:** 6| **Preparation Period:** 10 mins.| **Cooking Period:** 15 mins.

**Ingredients Required:**

- 8 C. water
- 1 (4-inch) piece ginger root (fresh), cut up
- 4 lemons, slivered
- 6 cardamom pods, bruised
- 1 cinnamon stick
- 1 whole star anise pod
- 3 tbsp. raw honey

**Procedure of Cooking:**

1. In a saucepan, put in water on burner at around medium-high heat
2. Cook the water until boiling.
3. Blend in ginger, lemon slices and spices and immediately turn the heat at around medium-low.
4. Cook for around 5-10 minutes.
5. Strain the tea into a pitcher.
6. Blend in honey and enjoy.

**Nutritional Facts:**
Calories: 37| Fat: 0.1g| Carbs: 10.1g| Protein: 0.2g

## Black Tea

**Serving Portion:** 2| **Preparation Period:** 5 mins.| **Cooking Period:** 5 mins.

**Ingredients Required:**

- 2 C. water
- 1-2 tsp. loose leaf black tea
- 2 teaspoons honey

**Procedure of Cooking:**

1. In a small-sized saucepan, put in water.
2. Cook the water until boiling.
3. Blend in in tea and turn off the heat.
4. Immediately cover the pan for 2-minutes.
5. Blend in honey and enjoy hot.

**Nutritional Facts:**
Calories: 1| Fat: 0g| Carbs: 2.2g| Protein: 1g

## Black Coffee

**Serving Portion:** 1| **Preparation Period:** 5 mins.

**Ingredients Required:**

- ½ tbsp. coffee powder
- 1-2 tsp. honey
- 1 C. boiling water

**Procedure of Cooking:**

1. In a mug, put in coffee, honey and boiling water and blend to incorporate thoroughly.
2. Enjoy hot.

**Nutritional Facts:**
Calories: 3| Fat: 0g| Carbs: 0.6g| Protein: 0.2g

# Sauces, Dressings & Condiments Recipes

## Cherry & Cranberry Sauce

**Serving Portions:** 8 | **Preparation Period:** 10 mins. | **Cooking Period:** 10 mins.

**Ingredients Required:**

- 6 oz. frozen cherries
- 6 oz. frozen cranberries
- ½ tsp. ginger root (fresh), finely cut up
- ¾ C. apple juice (fresh)
- 1 pinch of salt
- ¼ tsp. powdered cinnamon
- 1-2 tbsp. maple syrup

**Procedure of Cooking:**

1. In a saucepan, blend all together cherries, cranberries, ginger, apple juice and salt on burner at around high heat.
2. Cook the mixture until boiling.
3. Immediately turn the heat at around medium.
4. Cook for around 8-10 minutes, mixing time to time.
5. Blend in cinnamon and maple syrup and take off from burner.

**Nutritional Facts:**
Calories: 54 | Fat: 0.1g | Carbs: 12.3g | Protein: 0.1g

## Tomato Sauce

**Serving Portions:** 24 | **Preparation Period:** 15 mins. | **Cooking Period:** 50 mins.

**Ingredients Required:**

- 18 plum tomatoes, halved

- ½ of bell pepper, seeds removed and halved
- ½ of red onion, halved
- ½ of sweet onion, halved
- 1 medium-sized shallot, halved
- 2 tbsp. olive oil
- 3 tsp. basil (dried), divided
- 1 tbsp. applesauce
- 2 tsp. oregano (dried)
- 2 tsp. onion powder
- 1/8 tsp. powdered cayenne pepper

**Procedure of Cooking:**

1. For preheating: set your oven at 400°F.
2. Line a large-sized baking tray with baking paper.
3. In a large-sized bowl, put in tomatoes, bell pepper, onions, shallot, oil, 1 tsp. of basil and 1 tsp. of salt and toss it all to mingle nicely.
4. Lay out the vegetables onto the baking tray, cut side down.
5. Roast in your oven for around 30 minutes, flipping the vegetables once halfway through.
6. Take off the baking tray from oven and put it aside to cool slightly.
7. In a high-power mixer, put in roasted vegetables and process on high speed to form a smooth mixture.
8. In a saucepan, put in pureed vegetables and remnant ingredients on burner at around low heat.
9. Cook for around 19-20 minutes.
10. Take off from burner and put it aside to cool thoroughly before enjoying.

**Nutritional Facts:**
Calories: 33 | Fat: 1.3g | Carbs: 5.3g | Protein: 0.9g

# BBQ Sauce

**Serving Portions:** 12 | **Preparation Period:** 15 mins. | **Cooking Period:** 1 hr. 5 mins.

**Ingredients Required:**

- 16 oz. homemade tomato sauce
- ½ C. apple cider vinegar
- 5 tbsp. maple syrup
- 2 tbsp. tomato paste
- 1 tbsp. lemon juice (fresh)
- ½ tbsp. powdered mustard
- ½ tbsp. onion powder
- ½ tbsp. powdered black pepper
- 1 tsp. paprika
- 1 C. water

**Procedure of Cooking:**

1. In a medium-sized saucepan, blend all together tomato sauce and remnant ingredients on burner at around medium-high heat.
2. Cook the mixture until boiling..
3. Immediately turn the heat at around low.
4. Cook for around 1 hour.
5. Take off the saucepan of sauce from burner and shift into an airtight container.
6. Put it aside to cool thoroughly before storing in the refrigerator.

**Nutritional Facts:**
Calories: 40 | Fat: 0.3g | Carbs: 8.9g | Protein: 0.8g

# Herbed Parmesan Dip

**Serving Portions:** 12 | **Preparation Period:** 10 mins.

**Ingredients Required:**

- 1 C. parsley (fresh)

- 1 C. basil leaves (fresh)
- 2 cloves garlic, cut up
- ½ C. low-fat Parmesan cheese, grated
- ½ C. olive oil

**Procedure of Cooking:**

1. In a clean food mixer, put in herbs, garlic, Parmesan cheese and oil and process to form a smooth mixture.
2. Enjoy immediately.

**Nutritional Facts:**
Calories: 97 | Fat: 10.1g | Carbs: 0.7g | Protein: 1.9g

# Salsa Verde Dip

**Serving Portions:** 8 | **Preparation Period:** 15 mins. | **Cooking Period:** 40 mins.

**Ingredients Required:**

- 2 lb. medium tomatillos, husks removed and halved
- 2 large-sized sweet onions, roughly cut up
- 6 cloves garlic, peel removed and halved
- 2 Serrano peppers, seeds removed and cut up
- ¼ C. olive oil
- 1/3-½ C. water
- ½ C. cut up cilantro (fresh)
- 2 tbsp. lime juice (fresh)
- 1 pinch of salt

**Procedure of Cooking:**

1. For preheating: set your oven at 425°F.
2. In a large-sized bowl, put in tomatillos, onions, garlic, peppers and oil and toss it all to mingle nicely.
3. Divide tomatillo mixture onto 2 baking trays and then arrange in an even layer.
4. Roast in your oven for around 35-40 minutes, mixing time to time.

5. Take off the baking trays of tomatillo mixture from oven and put it aside to cool slightly.
6. In a clean food mixer, put in tomatillo mixture and enough water and process to form a smooth mixture.
7. Put in remnant ingredients and process until just combined.

**Nutritional Facts:**
Calories: 110| Fat: 7.5g| Carbs: 11g| Protein: 1.7g

## Cauliflower Hummus Dip

**Serving Portions:** 6| **Preparation Period:** 15 mins.| **Cooking Period:** 15 mins.

**Ingredients Required:**

- 3 C. cauliflower florets
- 6 tbsp. olive oil, divided
- 2 tbsp. water
- 3 whole cloves garlic, peel removed
- 3 tbsp. lemon juice (fresh)
- 1½ tbsp. tahini paste
- 2 cloves garlic, cut up
- Smoked paprika, for decoration

**Procedure of Cooking:**

1. In a large-sized microwave-safe bowl, blend all together cauliflower, 2 tbsp. of oil, water and whole cloves of garlic.
2. Microwave on high for around 15 minutes, mixing time to time.
3. Shift the cauliflower mixture into a high-power mixer and process to form a smooth mixture.
4. Put in 4 tbsp. of remnant oil, lemon juice, tahini and cut up garlic and process to form a smooth mixture.
5. Shift the hummus into a serving bowl.
6. Drizzle with remnant 1 tbsp. of oil and sprinkle with smoked paprika before enjoying.

**Nutritional Facts:**

Calories: 160| Fat: 16.1g| Carbs: 4.4g| Protein: 1.9g

## Lemony Garlic Dressing

**Serving Portions:** 6| **Preparation Period:** 10 mins.

**Ingredients Required:**

- 3 cloves garlic, finely cut up
- ½ C. extra-virgin olive oil
- ½ C. lemon juice (fresh)
- 1 pinch of salt
  Powdered black pepper, as desired

**Procedure of Cooking:**

1. In a large-sized bowl, put in garlic and remnant ingredients and whisk to incorporate thoroughly.
2. Enjoy immediately.

**Nutritional Facts:**
Calories: 168| Fat: 18.7g| Carbs: 8g| Protein: 0.2g

## Avocado & Cilantro Dressing

**Serving Portions:** 8| **Preparation Period:** 10 mins.

**Ingredients Required:**

- ¾ C. cilantro (fresh), cut up
- ½ of medium avocado, peel removed, pitted and cut up
- 2 medium-sized onions, cut up
- 1 clove garlic, cut up
- ¼ C. coconut milk (unsweetened)
- 1/3 C. olive oil
- 2 tbsp. lime juice (fresh)
- ½ tsp. salt
- ½ tsp. powdered black pepper

**Procedure of Cooking:**

1. In a high-power mixer, put in cilantro and remnant ingredients and process to form a smooth mixture.
2. Shift the dressing into an airtight jar and store in the refrigerator.

**Nutritional Facts:**
Calories: 136| Fat: 13.4g| Carbs: 4.4g| Protein: 0.8g

## Carrot Dressing

**Serving Portions:** 6| **Preparation Period:** 10 mins.

**Ingredients Required:**

- ¼ C. onion, cut up
- ¼ cu carrot, peel removed and cut up
- 1 tbsp. celery stalk, cut up
- 1 clove garlic, cut up
- 1 tbsp. ginger root (fresh), cut up
- 1 tbsp. tomato paste
- 3 tbsp. balsamic vinegar
- 1 tsp. lemon juice (fresh)
- 1 pinch of salt
- Powdered black pepper, as desired

**Procedure of Cooking:**

1. In a clean food mixer, put in onion and remnant ingredients and process to form a smooth mixture.

2. Shift into your refrigerator for 2-3 hours before enjoying.

**Nutritional Facts:**
Calories: 80| Fat: 6.8g| Carbs: 5.6g| Protein: 0.4g

## Raspberry Dressing

**Serving Portions:** 8| **Preparation Period:** 10 mins.

**Ingredients Required:**

- ½ C. raspberries (fresh)
- ½ C. olive oil
- 2 tbsp. balsamic vinegar
- 1 tsp. pure maple syrup
- 1 tsp. mustard
- 1 pinch of salt
- 1 tsp. powdered black pepper

**Procedure of Cooking:**

1. In a high-power mixer, put in strawberries and process to form a smooth pure.
2. Put in remnant ingredients and process to form a smooth mixture and creamy.
3. Shift the dressing into an airtight jar and store in the refrigerator.

**Nutritional Facts:**
Calories: 116| Fat: 12.8g| Carbs: 1.6g| Protein: 2.1g

# Dessert Recipes

## Fruity Yogurt Parfait

**Serving Portions:** 4 | **Preparation Period:** 15 minutes | **Cooking Period:** 10 minutes

**Ingredients Required:**

- 2 C. fat-free plain Greek yogurt
- ¼ C. honey
- ¼ C. water
- ½ tsp. fresh lime zest, finely grated
- ¼ tsp. powdered cinnamon
- ¼ tsp. vanilla extract
- 2 peaches, pitted and quartered
- 4 plums, pitted and quartered
- ¼ C. almonds, toasted and cut up

**Procedure of Cooking:**

1. In a medium-sized glass bowl, put in yogurt and honey and blend to incorporate thoroughly.
2. In a saucepan, blend all together the remnant ingredients except for almonds on burner at around medium heat.
3. Cook for around 8-10 minutes, mixing time to time.
4. Take off from burner and put it aside to cool.
5. Divide half of the yogurt mixture into 4 tall serving glasses.
6. Divide the fruit mixture over yogurt and top each with the remnant yogurt.
7. Decorate with almonds and enjoy.

**Nutritional Facts:**
Calories: 269 | Fat: 4.9g | Carbs: 48.5g | Protein: 9.5g

## Pineapple Sticks

**Serving Portions:** 8 | **Preparation Period:** 10 minutes

**Ingredients Required:**

- ¼ C. orange juice (fresh)
- ¾ C. unsweetened coconut, shredded and toasted
- 8 (3x1-inch) fresh pineapple pieces

**Procedure of Cooking:**

1. Lay out a wax paper onto a baking tray.
2. In a shallow basin, put in pineapple juice.
3. In another shallow basin, put in coconut.
4. Insert 1 wooden skewer in each pineapple piece from the narrow end.
5. Dip each pineapple piece in juice and then coat with coconut.
6. Lay out the pineapple sticks onto prepared baking tray in a single layer.
7. Cover and shift into your refrigerator for around 1-2 hours before enjoying.

**Nutritional Facts:**
Calories: 58 | Fat: 2.6g | Carbs: 9.4g | Protein: 0.6g

## Cinnamon Peaches

**Serving Portions:** 2 | **Preparation Period:** 10 minutes | **Cooking Period:** 10 minutes

**Ingredients Required:**

- Olive oil baking spray
- 2 medium-sized peaches, halved and pitted
- 1/8 tsp. powdered cinnamon

**Procedure of Cooking:**

1. For preheating: set your grill to medium-low heat.
2. Spray the grill grate with baking spray.
3. Lay out the peach slices onto the grill, cut-side down.
4. Cook for around 3-5 minutes from both sides.
5. Sprinkle with cinnamon and enjoy.

**Nutritional Facts:**
Calories: 60 | Fat: 0.4g | Carbs: 14.2g | Protein: 1.4g

## Lemon Sorbet

**Serving Portions:** 4 | **Preparation Period:** 10 minutes

**Ingredients Required:**

- 2 tbsp. fresh lemon zest, grated
- ½ C. pure maple syrup
- 2 C. water
- 1½ C. lemon juice (fresh)

**Procedure of Cooking:**

1. Freeze ice cream maker tub for around 24 hours before making this sorbet.
2. Put in all of the ingredients except the lemon juice in a saucepan.
3. Cook them on burner at around medium heat for around 1 minute or until the sugar dissolves, mixing all the time.
4. Take off the pan from burner and blend in the lemon juice.
5. Shift the mixture into an airtight container and shift into your refrigerator for around 2 hours.
6. Now, shift the mixture into an ice cream maker and process it according to the manufacturer's directions.
7. Return the ice cream to the airtight container and freeze for around 2 hours.

**Nutritional Facts:**
Calories: 127 | Fat: 0.8g | Carbs: 29g | Protein: 0.8g

## Spinach Sorbet

**Serving Portions:** 4 | **Preparation Period:** 15 minutes

**Ingredients Required:**

- 3 C. spinach (fresh), torn
- 1 tbsp. basil leaves (fresh)
- ½ of avocado, peel removed, pitted and cut up
- ¾ C. almond milk (unsweetened)
- 3-5 tbsp., maple syrup
- 1 tsp. almonds, cut up very finely
- 1 tsp. vanilla extract
- 1 C. ice cubes

**Procedure of Cooking:**

1. In a high-power mixer, put in spinach and remnant ingredients and process to form a creamy and smooth mixture.
2. Transfer into an ice cream maker and process according to manufacturer's directions.
3. Transfer into an airtight container and freeze for at least 4-5 hours before enjoying.

**Nutritional Facts:**
Calories: 375 | Fat: 16g | Carbs: 5.7g | Protein: 2.3g

## Pumpkin & Dates Ice Cream

**Serving Portions:** 8 | **Preparation Period:** 10 minutes

**Ingredients Required:**

- 1 (15-oz.) can sugar-free pumpkin puree
- ½ C. dates, pitted and cut up

- 2 (14-oz.) cans coconut milk (unsweetened)
- ½ tsp. vanilla extract
- 1½ tsp. pumpkin pie spice
- ½ tsp. powdered cinnamon
- 1 pinch of salt

**Procedure of Cooking:**

1. In a high-power mixer, put in pumpkin puree and remnant ingredients and process to form a smooth mixture.
2. Transfer into an airtight container and freeze for around 1-2 hours.
3. Now, transfer into an ice-cream maker and process according to manufacturer's directions.
4. Return the ice cream into airtight container and freeze for around 1-2 hours.

**Nutritional Facts:**
Calories: 200 | Fat: 13.9g | Carbs: 15.5g | Protein: 2.1g

---

# Raspberry Jelly

**Serving Portions:** 4 | **Preparation Period:** 10 minutes | **Cooking Period:** 40 minutes

**Ingredients Required:**

- 2 lb. raspberries (fresh)
- ¼ C. water
- 1 tbsp. lemon juice (fresh)

**Procedure of Cooking:**

1. In a medium-sized pan, put in raspberries and water on burner at around low heat.
2. Cook for 8-10 minutes, mixing time to time.
3. Put in lemon juice.
4. Cook for around 30 minutes.
5. Take off from burner and place the mixture into a sieve.

6. Strain the mixture into a bowl by pressing with the back of a spoon.
7. Now, shift the mixture into a mixer and process to form a jelly like texture.
8. Shift the jelly into glass serving bowls.
9. Shift the bowls into your refrigerator for at least 1 hour before enjoying.

**Nutritional Facts:**
Calories: 119 | Fat: 1.5g | Carbs: 27.2g | Protein: 2.8g

---

# Raspberry Brownies

**Serving Portions:** 10
| **Preparation Period:** 15 minutes
| **Cooking Period:** 22 minutes

**Ingredients Required:**

- Olive oil baking spray
- 1 tbsp. flaxseed meal
- 2½ tbsp. water
- ¼ C. plus 2 tbsp. dark unsweetened chocolate chips, divided
- 2 tbsp. coconut oil
- ¼ C. gluten-free rolled oats
- ½ C. unsweetened chocolate protein powder
- ½ C. cacao powder
- 2/3 C. unsweetened almond milk
- ½ C. unsweetened applesauce
- 1 tbsp. maple syrup
- 1 tsp. vanilla extract
- ½ C. raspberries (fresh), broken up into large pieces

**Procedure of Cooking:**

1. For preheating: set your oven at 350°F.
2. Spray an 8x8-inch baking pan with baking spray.
3. In a large-sized bowl, put in ground flax and water and blend to incorporate thoroughly.
4. Put it aside for around 5 minutes

5. In a microwave-safe bowl, put in ¼ C. of chocolate chips and coconut oil.
6. Microwave on High for around 1 minute, mixing after every 20 seconds.
7. Take off the bowl of chocolate mixture from microwave and stir until just smooth.
8. Place oats in a clean mixer and process to form a flour-like texture.
9. In a large-sized bowl, put in oat flour, protein powder and cacao powder and blend to incorporate thoroughly.
10. In the bowl of flaxseed mixture, put in almond milk, applesauce, maple syrup and vanilla extract and whisk to form a smooth mixture.
11. Put in flour mixture into the bowl of flaxseed mixture and mix until just blended.
12. Put in chocolate chips mixture and lightly blend to incorporate.
13. Place the brownie mixture into the baking pan and with the back of a spoon, smooth the top surface.
14. Place the remnant chocolate chips and raspberries on top and with a knife, swirl them in the mixture.
15. Bake in your oven for around 18-22 minutes.
16. Take off the baking pan from oven and place onto a wire rack to cool.
17. Divide into serving brownies and enjoy.

**Nutritional Facts:**
Calories: 119 | Fat: 6.2g | Carbs: 12.2g | Protein: 6.2g

---

## Blueberry Clafoutis

---

**Serving Portions:** 6 | **Preparation Period:** 15 minutes | **Cooking Period:** 22 minutes

**Ingredients Required:**

- 1 tsp. coconut oil
- ½ C. whole-wheat flour
- 1/8 tsp. powdered cinnamon
- 1 pinch of sea salt

- 3 eggs
- ½ C. almond milk (unsweetened)
- 1 tbsp. coconut oil, liquefied
- 1 tsp. vanilla extract
- 2 C. blueberries (fresh)
- ¼ C. almonds, cut up

**Procedure of Cooking:**

1. For preheating: set your oven at 450°F.
2. In a 10-inch Dutch oven, put in 1 tsp. of coconut oil and place into the oven to preheat.
3. In a large-sized bowl, put in flour, cinnamon and salt and blend to incorporate thoroughly.
4. In a separate bowl, put in eggs, almond milk, liquefied coconut oil and vanilla extract and whisk to incorporate thoroughly.
5. Put in egg mixture into the bowl of flour mixture and blend to incorporate thoroughly.
6. Take off the Dutch oven from oven and tilt to spread the coconut oil.
7. Place blueberries in the bottom of pan in a single layer.
8. Place the flour mixture over blueberries and top with almonds.
9. Bake in your oven for around 16-20 minutes.
10. Take off the Dutch oven from oven and let it cool thoroughly before slicing.
11. Divide into serving wedges and enjoy.

**Nutritional Facts:**
Calories: 128 | Fat: 6.2g | Carbs: 16.3g | Protein: 5.1g

---

## Apple Crisp

---

**Serving Portions:** 10 | **Preparation Period:** 15 minutes | **Cooking Period:** 20 minutes

**Ingredients Required:**

**For the Filling:**

- 2 large-sized apples, peel removed, cored and cut up
- 2 tbsp. fresh apple juice
- 2 tbsp. water
- ¼ tsp. powdered cinnamon

**For the Topping:**

- ½ C. gluten-free quick-rolled oats
- 2 tbsp. unsalted walnuts, cut up
- ¼ C. coconut flakes (unsweetened)
- ½ tsp. powdered cinnamon
- ¼ C. water

**Procedure of Cooking:**

1. For preheating: set your oven at 300°F.
2. In a large-sized baking pan, put in all filling ingredients and gently mix.
3. In a bowl, put in all topping ingredients and blend to incorporate thoroughly.
4. Spread the topping over the filling mixture.
5. Bake in your oven for around 20 minutes.
6. Enjoy warm.

**Nutritional Facts:**
Calories: 93 | Fat: 3g | Carbs: 16.1g | Protein: 1.4g

# Conclusion

In conclusion, The Galveston Diet offers a comprehensive and effective solution for individuals experiencing pre-menopause, menopause, and beyond by focusing on an anti-inflammatory nutrition program. With its emphasis on reducing inflammation in the body, this diet not only addresses weight management but also addresses other health concerns commonly associated with hormonal changes during this stage of life. Furthermore, the program's supportive community provides invaluable resources and a sense of belonging, enhancing the overall experience and empowering individuals to navigate this transformative phase with confidence and improved well-being. The Galveston Diet stands as a holistic and empowering approach to nutrition and wellness for women in the perimenopause and menopause stages and beyond.

Made in the USA
Las Vegas, NV
30 September 2023

78175180R00059